British Pixies

John Kruse

GREEN MAGIC

British Pixies © 2021 by John Kruse. All rights reserved. No part of this book may be used or reproduced in any form without written permission of the author, except in the case of quotations in articles and reviews.

Green Magic
53 Brooks Road
Street
Somerset
BA16 0PP
England

www.greenmagicpublishing.com

Designed and typeset by K.DESIGN
Winscombe, Somerset

ISBN 9781838132484

GREEN MAGIC

Contents

Introduction	5
CHAPTER ONE Origins	9
Literary	9
Spiritual	13
CHAPTER TWO Appearance	18
Physique	18
Voices	20
Clothing	21
Shape Shifting	25
CHAPTER THREE Character	28
Privacy	29
Respect	32
Religion	34
Offerings	35
CHAPTER FOUR Places	37
Ancient Sites	37
Underground Dwellings	38
Human Habitations	40
CHAPTER FIVE Activities	42
Fairs and Markets	42
Dances, Music and Sports	45
Pixie Rings	47
Mines	48
Livestock	50
Flight	52

CHAPTER SIX Human Relations	54
Gold	55
Household Visitors	58
Household Help	59
Harvest and Threshing	62
Repairs	65
Catching	66
Pixy Sight	69
CHAPTER SEVEN Mischief	73
Pranks	74
Riding Horses	76
Gallitraps	79
Abductions	81
Changelings	85
Fighting	90
Smuggling	91
Weather	92
Protections	92
CHAPTER EIGHT Pixie Leading	94
Methods	94
Motivations	97
Reactions	98
Remedies	100
Summary	104
CHAPTER NINE Fading Belief?	105
Further Reading	108

Introduction

The pixies are the faery folk of the South West of England, by which I mean Cornwall, Devon and the western part of Somerset (essentially Exmoor, the Quantocks and the Blackdown Hills). Beyond this area, moving into northern and eastern Somerset and into Dorset, it is far more common to speak of fairies. There are mentions of a being called the *cole-pexy* in Dorset, who is said to live in woods, caves or bogs (like the westerly pixies) whereas the *colt-pixy* of Hampshire is reported to take the form of a horse and protects orchards from thieves. Information about these latter creatures is regrettably limited.[1]

Regarding terminology, usage of the dialectical variants piskies, pisgies or pigsies, is common in the South West, but for simplicity this book will use the most commonly recognised term pixie/pixies. There is no material difference between a pisky, a pisgie and a pixie, but in considering Cornwall, we must confront a much more significant problem. Several writers, most notably Robert Hunt in his *Popular Romances of the West of England* (1865), have stated that five sub-divisions of the supernatural population of the county are "clearly distinguishable."

---

[1] 'New Forest and Local Superstitions,' *Southampton Herald*. May 27th 1893, 2.

Firstly, there are the 'little people', called the *pobel vean* in Cornish and described as innocent and beautiful. There are also, of course, the pixies, but from time to time we'll also hear of *spriggans*. These don't appear to be an entirely different type of creature – just a permanently bad-tempered and nasty pixie. They are described as being dour and ugly, mischievous and thievish; their particular role seems to be protecting other pixies from intrusions or insults by humankind (see, for example, the stories of *The Miser on the Faery Gump* or *The Faeries on the Eastern Green*, both from Penwith in West Cornwall). The spriggans are very closely linked to ancient sites, such as hill-forts, where they guard buried gold. According to one account, the spriggans are the ghosts of giants and are warrior sprites who can change their size. On this basis, certainly, they would seem not to be pixies at all. Enys Tregarthen, a Cornish fairy tale writer, certainly was of this opinion: she stated that the spriggans had turned the pixies out of the *googs* (caverns) where they had lived at Polzeath Bay. She regarded the former as akin to the hobgoblins of England.[2]

Folklore writer Margaret Courtney distin-guished between the *pobel vean*, who associate in groups, and the solitary pixies, who are reported to be seen in parties of no more than two or three. More recently, Tony Deane and Tony Shaw expressed the opinion that there were only three categories of fairy being in Cornwall – the knockers, the brownies and the *pobel vean*. Enys Tregarthen, who was just mentioned, considered that the

---

2 W. Bottrell, *Stories and Folklore of West Cornwall*, 194; Deane and Shaw, *Folklore of Cornwall*, 1975, 95; E. Tregarthen, *Pisky Purse*, 1905.

'wee folk' comprised the pixies and the 'night riders' (the fairy folk who take horses from stables and ride them). She further distinguished the 'merry little people' and the 'bad little people,' the latter being spiteful lovers of gold.[3]

There are certainly some reports of domestic sprites, who live in people's homes and perform household tasks for them. Without question, these individuals begin to shade into 'brownies' but, despite what Deane and Shaw suggested, there doesn't seem to be a separate species of brownie as is identified in much of England or southern Scotland. Instead, we seem here to be dealing with pixies that have chosen to take up residence in human homes and other buildings.

To complicate matters yet further, there's a being called the *bucca* which Hunt seems to treat as being the same as the much more famous 'knockers' who are found in mines, while Bottrell at one point uses *bucca* interchangeably with both *piskey* and with *pobel vean*. On farms, it used to be said, when the milk went sour, that there was "the Buck in the dairy." Walter Evans Wentz, meanwhile, was told in 1910 by one of his Cornish witnesses that the *bucca* was just another name for a 'sea-strand' pixie. Yet another account described the *bucca* as a being very much resembling a merman, who may be seen swimming along the sea bed by fishing crews. William Bottrell uses the word *bucca* as an alternative for changeling.[4]

---

3   M. Courtney, *Cornish Feasts and Folklore*, 1890, 122; Deane and Shaw, *Folklore of Cornwall*, 1975, 84; E. Tregarthen, *Pisky Purse*, 1905.
4   'Old Cornwall – Concerning Fairies,' *Royal Cornwall Gazette*, Jan. 12th 1883, 6; Bottrell, *Traditions and Hearthside Stories*, vol.2, 163 and 202 and *Stories and Folklore of West Cornwall*,

Then again, certain writers seem to imply that the terminology doesn't reflect any profound difference in either form *or* temperament. For example, a Cornish historian in 1824 referred generally to "fairies, sprites, spriggians, gentle people, good people or piskays," a catch-all sentence that appears to lump identical beings together.[5]

To summarise, the difference between all of these faeries – if there is any at all – is far from certain. Given the inconsistency with which the terms are used by earlier folklorists, which may be directly reflective of the imprecise language of their interviewees, it is probably not justifiable to insist upon strict boundaries between most of the different classes of Cornish faery that have been identified. It seems likely that pixies, spriggans, knockers and the *pobel vean* are all simply pixie folk, differentiated solely by the location in which they tend to be found. For instance, we might call them knockers down mines and spriggans if we encountered them at an ancient site but, ultimately, they are all just representatives of the small folk of the South West of Britain. There may be more reason for separating out the *bucca* and regarding him as something like the English hob or boggart, but this is far from certain.

In conclusion, we should bear in mind that in many respects the conduct of the pixies resembles exactly that of the elves and fairies of the rest of Britain and, as a consequence, exactly the same stories are told about them. Nonetheless, the pixies have unique features to their behaviour which make a separate treatment worthwhile.

93; W. Evans Wentz, *The Fairy Faith in Celtic Countries,* 1911, 175; J. Harris, *Cornish Saints and Sinners,* 1907, c.31 (see too my *Beyond Faery,* 2020).
5   S. F. Hitchens, *History of Cornwall,* 1824, vol.1, 97.

CHAPTER ONE

Origins

Pixies came to wider attention through the work of a handful of authors. Before that, they had been well-known within the south-west, and local people had speculated about their origins over centuries.

Literary

Writing his *Song of the Pixies* in 1793, Samuel Taylor Coleridge provided one of the first printed references to the fairy tribe. He described how they would retreat to a shady hollow before sun rose, lest "our filmy pinion/ We scorch amid the blaze of day." His pixies were a "race of beings invisibly small and harmless and friendly to man" and it is clear from the preface to his work that, at the date he wrote, Coleridge didn't expect anyone outside Devonshire to have heard of these south western entities.

It is evident from Coleridge's poem that pixies were well known in the south-west, but they only really came to national attention around four decades later, when a Mrs Anna Bray published the first of several books on them, *A Description of the Part of Devonshire Bordering on the Tamar and Tavy* (1836). She introduced readers to a very particular vision of the species; as her correspondent Southey wrote to her in December 1832, "Your pixies are pleasant creatures." So popular was Mrs Bray's first book that she followed it up with a text specifically aimed at children, *Peeps at Pixies* of 1854. Certainly, Mrs Bray's pixies were extraordinarily influential, and her image of tiny playful beings with pointed ears very quickly became ubiquitous in Victorian and Edwardian children's book illustrations and established a cultural convention that persists today. Consider, for example, Julius Madison Cawein's *Pixy Wood,* in which cups of fungus form casks of wine for elvish moonlit revels, or James Whitcomb Riley's *Pixy People* in which winged pixies are seen "Pouring from the steeple/ Of a mullein stalk."[6]

The pixies were quickly taken up by many other writers. A curious illustration of this is a paragraph of juvenilia from the family journal, 'The Rectory Umbrella,' which was 'published' by Lewis Carroll (Charles Dodgson) and his brothers and sisters between 1850 and 1853. The journal was written entirely for their own amusement, but it is of interest not just because it foreshadows the fantasy fiction of the Alice stories but because it demonstrates the impact of Mrs Bray's work upon Victorian conceptions of fairyland.

Carroll's pixie text appears under the sub-title: 'Zoological papers' and makes fun of the learned scientific, academic style, with its use of footnotes and citations from other authorities.

> "The origin of this curious race of creatures is not at present known: the best description we can collect of them is this, that they are a species of fairies

---

[6] See P. Manwaring, 'The Pixies' Progress – how Pixies became Part of Nineteenth century *Fairy Mythology.*'

about two feet high (1), of small and graceful figure; they are covered in a dark reddish kind of fur; the general expression of their faces is sweetness and good humour; the former quality is probably the reason why foxes are so fond of eating them. From Coleridge we learn the following additional facts; that they have 'filmy pinions' something like dragon flies' wings, that they 'sip the furze-flower's fragrant dew' (that, however, could only be for breakfast, as it would dry up before dinner-time), and that they are wont to 'flash their faery feet in gamesome prank,' or, in more common language, 'to dance the polka (2) like winking.'

From an old English legend (3) which, as it is familiar with our readers, we need not here repeat, we learn that they have a strong affection for raw turnips, decidedly a more vulgar sort of food than 'fragrant dew;' and from their using churns and kettles we conjecture that they are not unacquainted with tea, milk, butter andc. They are tolerably good architects, though their houses must unavoidably have something the appearance of large dog kennels, and they go to market occasionally, though from what source they get the money for this purpose has hitherto remained an unexplained mystery. This is all the information we have been able to collect on this interesting subject.

(1) So they are described by the inhabitants of Devonshire, who occasionally see them.
(2) Or any other step.
(3) A tradition, introduced into notice by the Editor."

It seems very likely that the Dodgson family must have been familiar with Mrs Bray.

Carroll's fairy lore, meanwhile, is on the whole sound (excepting, that is, the diet of turnips... as he confessed himself). As shall be seen later in chapter four, there was indeed a longstanding animosity between the Dartmoor foxes and pixies, which led to an ever-increasing effort by the latter to protect themselves. We know too of fairies' partiality for dairy products and it had long been a poetic conceit that the tiny rural beings would drink dew and nectar from flowers. We are also very familiar with their love of dancing. Their use of kettles and the like is quite conventional and, as we shall see, one common set of stories from across Britain involves fairies seeking human aid to mend some basic item of domestic equipment. Tales of fairies at markets are also well-known, although their habit is often to thieve from the stalls rather than to buy. Fairies often had gold, it is true, which tended to be used to make gifts to chosen favourites rather than to purchase goods, and many writers speculated about its source.

Carroll's pixies coincided very much with broader fairy tradition, then, and even his jokey invention of their foxy fur coats is not entirely unheard of, as a couple of more contemporary sightings have shown. The description of the pixies as always jolly is surprising though because, as many readers may already know, they have a great tendency to mischief – hence the term 'pixy-led.'

On a rather loftier literary plane, Thomas Hardy made reference to pixy-leading in Dorset in the third chapter of *The Return of the Native* (1878); later Algernon Blackwood, a writer of mystery and horror short stories, used the same idea in *Entrance and Exit* of 1914 and in *May Day Eve*, published in 1907. The latter is a detailed account of a rational medical man being pixy-led on his way to visit an old friend, a folklorist, in his moorland home. A mist descends and the doctor becomes lost and panicked, overcome with a sense that the landscape around him is alive. He comes upon a cottage filled with strange people before finally picking up the path to his friend's house again. The folklorist calls the people his friend encountered 'elemental beings,' and explains that he has been wrapped in glamour whilst venturing out on May Day Eve, one of the most perilous nights of the year. The whole story is a wonderful mix of terror, bewilderment, mystery and wonder, a memorable evocation of what it must feel like to be pixy-led.

Spiritual

Since at least the nineteenth century there has been considerable speculation about the physical and spiritual place of pixies in the Christian cosmos. A number of competing theories have been put forward. Opinion was likewise divided over what, if anything, the pixies themselves believed in.

Mrs Bray suggested that the pixies had been amongst the deities worshipped by the druids, but she also suggested that they were the souls of children who died unbaptised. It seems very likely that she borrowed the druid idea from eighteenth century Cornish writer William Borlase. He believed that the druids had worshipped rocks and springs and other natural features and that they also imagined these to be inhabited by "divine intelligences of a lower rank." Borlase then went on to state that these "inferior deities the Cornish call Spriggian, or Spirits; they answer to the Genii or Fairies of the ancients, and of these the vulgar in Cornwall still discourse as of real beings, attribute to them large powers to rule the weather and to discover hidden treasures, and pay them a kind of veneration." What Borlase meant by this is made clearer in a history of Cornwall published in 1824, in which the author described how "some degrees of veneration" were still attached to the places believed to be frequented by the piskies – lanes, fields, bushes and hedges. "An indefinite species of sanctity is still associated with their beaten circles and it is thought unlucky to injure their haunts or throw any obstacle in their way."[7]

Collecting evidence on Cornish pixie beliefs towards the end of the first decade of the twentieth century, Walter Evans Wentz was offered a variety of conceptions of their nature. Witnesses told him that the pixies were the spirits of the dead or ghosts, the souls of the prehistoric residents of the county, spirits of nature inherited from the Celtic people or the souls of still born (and therefore unbaptised) children. The association of the pixies with standing stones, long barrows and stone circles must naturally have reinforced some of these ideas. Evans Wentz was also told in 1910 that miners believed white moths to be spirits and this is reflective of

---

7   Bray, *Description,* I, 171 and 172; Borlase, *Antiquities, Historical and Monumental, of the County of Cornwall,* 1769, 110; Borlase, *Antiquities, Historical and Monumental, of the County of Cornwall,* 1769, 110; S. F. Hitchens, *History of Cornwall,* vol.1, 97.

a wider association between the insects and the pixies.[8]

Our starting point in examining this connection is a brief remark by Robert Hunt in his *Popular Romances of the West of England*:

> "Mr Thoms has noticed that in Cornwall 'the moths which some regard as departed souls, others as fairies, are called *Pisgies*.' This is somewhat too generally expressed; the belief respecting the moth, so far as I know, is confined to one or two varieties only. Mr Couch informs us that the local name, around Polperro, of the weasel is *Fairy*. So that we have evidence of some sort of metempsychosis amongst the elf family. Moths, ants, and weasels it would seem are the forms taken by those wandering spirits."[9]

The Mr Thoms mentioned by Hunt wrote about 'The Folklore of Shakespeare' in *The Athenaeum* in 1847. In this article he said little more than Hunt repeated, except to say that the identity of moths with pixies was a belief found in the Truro area of mid-Cornwall, adding that it was thought that when the moths were very numerous, there would be great mortality to follow.[10]

There are some other fragments of folk belief to add to these tantalising remnants. According to J. Henry Harris, Cornish mothers would also tell their children that the little brown pisgie moth would play tricks on them in their sleep. At St Nun's Well near Looe on the south coast of the Cornish peninsula, there is a tradition of leaving

---

8 Wentz, *Fairy Faith*, 171, 172, 174, 176, 178, 179 and 183.
9 *Popular Romances of the West of England*, 1865, 82.
10 *Athenaeum*, no.1041, 1055.

a bent pin as an offering. If you fail to do this, you will be followed home by a cloud of the pisgey moths. Fairies are often linked with wells and this particular local tradition demonstrates that the same connection existed in Cornwall and the need to show proper respect by making respectful offerings to the fairies.[11]

Lastly, in a story from the Blackdown Hills of Somerset, a woman who was brushed across her brow by a large moth thereby received the 'pixy-sight' which enabled her to see an old pixy man who had come to ask for her skill in nursing his sick wife. We know faery powers generally can be transferred by touch, so this again fits in with wider lore, although the medium of the moth is unusual.

The Cornish tradition that brambles shouldn't be gathered and eaten after Halloween seems to be related to beliefs about the spiritual identity of the pixies. It is said that they are no longer fit to eat because the pixies have been "over them." This phrase seems to be a polite way of saying that the fruit have been urinated upon, but in itself it makes little sense unless we also accept that there is a connection to the dead and even the devil implicit in the tradition.[12]

The consensus appears to have been that the pixies stood outside the Christian universe, possibly being opposed to it. Whether they were solely immaterial spirits or were flesh and blood beings was a great deal less certain. Jonathan Couch, describing the piskies of the southern Cornish coast in 1871, summarised them in the following terms: he said they are midway between spiritual and material and can be seen heard and felt

---

[11] Harris, *Cornish Saints and Sinners,* 1907, c.20.
[12] Wentz, *Fairy Faith*, 179.

by human beings. This tallies with a statement made to Evans Wentz by a Sennen fisherman, who believed that the pixies are "a sort of people wandering about the world without home or habitation [who] ought to be given a little comfort" by admission to human homes, most especially in bad weather. This certainly implies that they have physical bodies and are as susceptible to cold, wet and hunger as any human being. In the same vein, John Male of Delabole described the pixies as "a race of little people who live out in the fields." This definitely suggests isolation and exposure to the elements.[13]

---

13   J. Couch, *History of Polperro*, 1871, c.VII, 133; Wentz, *Fairy Faith*, 182 and 184.

CHAPTER TWO

Appearance

In 1836, Mrs Bray provided the first descriptions of the Dartmoor pixies, stating that some were notably beautiful and that others were distinctly ugly. They could shape shift and were 'always' to be seen dressed in green. In this chapter, we shall examine this earliest description of the pixie race in more detail.[14]

Physique

Starting in the east of the region covered by this study, the Somerset fairies are reported to be red-haired with pointed ears, having short faces and turned up noses. The Exmoor pixies have been compared in height to "little children."[15]

Heading south and west, the pixies of Dartmoor were described by Mrs Bray as being little creatures much smaller than children, who can get into flower bells and "many other places where girls and boys cannot creep," meaning that they can't be excluded from any place or container. Nevertheless, they can change their size, so that the pixies have also been estimated as being about eighteen inches tall on average, although heights from

---
14 Bray, *Description*, I, 173.
15 Tongue, *Somerset Folklore*, Folklore Society County Folklore vol.8, 1965, 113; Snell, *Book of Exmoor*, 1903, 255.

APPEARANCE

twelve inches to three feet have been reported. Because of their small size, they're often said to look like dolls. In another Devonshire tradition, the pixies were reported to be "slim and sprightly," again being between twelve inches and three feet in height.[16]

Mrs Bray said the Devonshire pixies could be "dainty beings ... of exceeding beauty [but that] others are of strange, uncouth and fantastic figure and visage." It's widely agreed that one of the distinguishing features of the pixies is their pronounced squint.[17]

The extreme tininess of at least some Cornish pixies may be indicated by the fact that gnats are sometimes referred to as 'piskies.' In one of her stories, writer Enys Tregarthen described some pixies doing housework as being "not much bigger than clothes pegs, and all as busy as a flock of starlings in a stubble field." She also made the fascinating statement that the pixies show their age by getting younger and fairer as time passes (or, at least, their royalty do this).[18]

Focussing on their facial features, pixies are quite often described as being weather beaten, sun-tanned and somewhat wrinkled. Nonetheless, one Cornish witness gave a more mixed account, describing the males as "swarthy in complexion, [whereas] the women had a clear complexion of peach-like bloom. None ever

---

16 A. Bray, *Peeps on pixies* (London, Grant and Griffith, 1854), 11; Page, *An Exploration of Dartmoor*, 1895, 39; W. Bottrell, *Traditions and Hearthside Stories* (Penzance, 1870) vol.1, 77; J. Coxhead, *Devon Traditions and Fairy Tales*, 1959, 49.
17 Bray, *Peeps on Pixies*,12; Charles Worthy, *Devonshire Parishes*, 1887, 28; Page, *Dartmoor*, 38.
18 'Old Cornwall – Concerning Fairies,' *Royal Cornwall Gazette*, Jan. 12th 1883, 6; E. Tregarthen, *Folklore Tales*, 2020, 'Curious Woman of Davidstow,' (1940); Pisky Purse, 1905.

appeared to be more than five and twenty to thirty years old."[19]

An old woman who came across a Halloween pixie fair at Pendeen in Penwith saw similar handsome crowds assembled. They were small:

> "none more than two feet high, and rather slender in make... The men were much darker complexioned than the women, yet they were all very good looking, with sparkling dark eyes, well-shaped noses, sweet little mouths, and dimpled cheeks and chins. Not one among them, that she saw, had a spotty face or purple-top nose, because they drink nothing stronger than honey-dew. Some, to be sure, appeared to be rather aged yet, all were sprightly, merry, and gay."[20]

Voices

Opinions on pixies' voices are rather contradictory. A Somerset farmer often heard the pixies when he was a boy early last century and his description was of "voices sort of near, sort of far, laughing, jesting, squabbling, even singing some strange songs in some queer language, like birds." Another time, the same man overheard the pixies threshing grain in his barn, singing as they worked in "croaky bird-like voices."[21]

Commensurate with their size, the pixies encountered on Silena Moor near St Buryan squeaked with little voices and some doll-like beings, seen dancing in a circle

---
19 Wentz, *Fairy Faith*, 177.
20 Bottrell, *Traditions and Hearthside Stories*, vol.2, 161.
21 *Somerset Fairies and Pixies* 101 and 106.

by a spring at Sennen in 1888, were reported to have squeaked like mice. These instances notwithstanding, the Reverend Hawker, in contrast to all the evidence so far, reported that the North Cornwall pixies could be heard singing in the evenings, "like a Christmas choir." Robert Hunt went so far as to say that the *pobel vean* celebrated Christmas with melodious singing "beyond all earthly voices." Indeed, in one of Enys Tregarthen's stories, a fairy child's singing (which isn't in the Cornish language) makes crockery and furniture dance.[22]

Clothing

Whilst there is, on the whole, considerable consensus about what pixies look like physically, reports of their clothing are much more mixed. Travelling again east to west, the Exmoor pixies are reported to be very prettily dressed and doubtless this adds to their attractiveness, given that they are said to look like infants. These Somerset pixies prefer to wear green.[23]

The South Devonshire pixies were also said to be (to wear?) green, a colour of which they are allegedly highly protective: the saying in the south of the county was that, if a human wears green, they'll soon be wearing mourning.[24]

An old Dartmoor woman, interviewed in the mid-1860s, said she had seen a pixie as a girl: he had been

---

22 Briggs, *Dictionary*, 142; R. Hawker, *Footprints of Former Men in Far Cornwall*; Hunt, *Popular Romances*, vol.2, 123; Tregarthen, *Folklore Tales*, 'Skerry Werry,' (1940).
23 Tongue, *Somerset Folklore*, 113; F. J. Snell, *Book of Exmoor*, 1903, 25.
24 'Folklore at Beesands,' *Folklore*, vol.27, 1916, 307.

about eighteen inches high, wearing a hat and holding a pipe and a jug. Another Dartmoor report puzzlingly states that the pixies may be naked, dressed in bright apparel or wearing only rags. Then again, a Mrs G. Herbert claimed to have glimpsed a pixie at Shaugh Bridge, on the south west edge of Dartmoor, in 1897. He was a little wrinkled and wizened man, between eighteen and twenty-four inches tall, dressed in a pointed hat, doublet and "short knicker things" coloured blue and red. Of course, he vanished as soon as she had caught sight of him.[25]

A pixie seen in 1952 at Haytor was about three feet high and dressed entirely in brown. A second modern Dartmoor sighting, recorded in 1960, reported that four pixies were witnessed coming out of a stack of bracken in a field. They were all male, with two being taller and less pleasant looking than their companions. They were each dressed in red doublets, red pointed caps and long green hose or stockings. Another contemporary report of a pixie seen at Fur Tor described him as being clad in 'ordinary' clothes – although he vanished as soon as he was spotted.[26]

Turning to Cornwall, the bulk of the reports on pixie clothing come from the far west, from Penwith. An old woman living at Penberth Cove characterised the male pixies there as looking like "little sodgers" (soldiers), dressed in green with feathered caps of red or blue. The women were more elaborately dressed, she said, in hooped petticoats with furbelows (pleated borders) and trains, fans and feathers. Elsewhere in Penwith, it

---

[25] Bowring, 'Devon Folklore,' 80; Coxhead, *Devon Traditions and Fairy Tales*, 49 and %1.
[26] R. St Leger Gordon, *The Witchcraft and Folklore of Dartmoor*, 1965, 21.

was stated in mid-Victorian times that the pixies were about the height of a candlestick and dressed in green, with a straw hat or red cap. The same applies to pixies at Polperro, who are a 'span' in height. Pixies seen dancing near Land's End were "like little children and had red cloaks."[27]

Fairies seen in a field near St Buryan in Penwith were said to be about a yard tall, the men looking like soldiers or huntsmen (that is, in red) and the women in "gowns as gay as a flower-garden in summer; [whose] flaxen hair fell in long curls on their necks."[28]

In 1830 a tailor of Sparnick in mid-Cornwall was walking home one night from Calenick when, upon reaching the church yard of St Kea, he saw a troop of pixies, about eighteen inches in height, cross the road in front of him and disappear into the church yard. They were dressed in red cloaks and wore tall, black sugar loaf hats of an old-fashioned style. Some North Cornwall pixies who pisky-led a man called Jan Brewer wore green coats and purple and black caps whilst the females had green cloaks with red hoods. Bottrell recorded that the *pobel vean* dressed in sky blue hats with green trousers; sometimes the men wore three cornered hats and the women were seen in very pointed headwear, all decorated with lace and silver bells.[29]

---

[27] Couch, 'Cornish Folklore,' *Penzance Natural History and Antiquarian Society Report*, in *Royal Cornwall Gazette*, Nov.11th, 1853, 6; J. Couch, *History of Polperro*, 134; Wentz, *Fairy Faith*, 142, 155 and 181.
[28] Bottrell, *Traditions and Hearthside Stories*, vol.2, 73.
[29] 'Common Antiquities and *Folklore of Cornwall*,' *Royal Cornwall Gazette*, December 19th 1879, 6; 'How Jan Brewer was Pisky Laden,' in Tregarthen, *North Cornwall Fairies and Legends*, 185; Bottrell, *Hearthside Tales*, 246.

Two girls from Sennen saw three of the *pobel vean* dancing beside a spring one moonlit night in August 1888. They described them as being:

> "dressed in a very thin white stuff like muslin, drawn in at the waist, and thrown all over their heads like a bride's veil – so that I could not see their faces – and coming down over their arms. Their arms were stretched out rather drooping from the shoulder, and their hands were joined. I saw their hands very plainly, but did not distinguish fingers. They were as white as snow, hands and all. They had very small waists, no larger than the neck of that jug [6.5 inches]. Their dresses swell[ed] out at the bottom from the dancing; they were very long, and I don't think I saw their feet, but they appeared to be dancing with a movement as though they were working their legs."[30]

Lastly, the old woman who came across the Halloween pixie fair at Pendeen saw crowds who were:

> "all decked out like old-fashioned gentry: the little men in three-cocked hats and feathers; full, square-skirted, blue coats, stiff with buckram and gay with lace and buttons; vest, breeches, and stockings of a lighter hue; and their dainty little shoes fastened with diamond clasps. Some few, who were rigged more like soldiers or huntsmen, wore either jet-black or russet-coloured riding boots.

---

30 E. Westlake, 'A Traditional Hallucination', *Journal of the Society for Psychic Research* vol. 11 (1904), 191–193.

An' Pee said that she couldn't name the colours of the little ladies' dresses, which were of all the hues of summer's blossoms. The vain little things, to make themselves look the taller, had their powdered hair turned up on pads and dressed with flowers, lace, and ribbons to an extraordinary height for such dolls of things. Their gay gowns were very long-waisted, and their skirts so distended by hoops that they looked just as broad as they were long. Their shoes of velvet or satin, were high-heeled and pointed at the toes."[31]

In conclusion, it is clear that green, along with red, are the preferred colours of pixie clothing (a taste which they share with the majority of British fairies), although more earthy shades are not unheard of amongst these moorland dwellers. The question of styles is a little more complicated, but the overall impression is that pixies are often sighted wearing garments that were fashionable at some point in the more or less distant past. The numerous references to cloaks demonstrate this, as do the descriptions of outfits that sound almost medieval. One thing is certain: even if they do resemble children in size, the anachronistic clothing may well give them away.

Shape Shifting

The pixies can reduce themselves to any size, so that they can get into any human property or escape from any confinement. More than that, they can transform their appearance entirely – and into quite surprising forms.[32]

---
31 Bottrell, *Traditions and Hearthside Stories*, vol.2, 161.
32 Page, *An Exploration of Dartmoor*, 39.

A boy lost on Dartmoor was found by his mother seated under an oak tree that was widely known to be a pixie haunt. He told her that "two bundles of rags" had led him away – evidently, pixies who were in disguise so as to attract his attention and lull his suspicions. As soon as the lights of his mother's lantern had appeared, these rags vanished. The Devon pixies have also been said to move around like "balls of fern or heather, swept before the wind" and, indeed, a Welsh brownie called the *pwcca* looks like a handful of grass blowing along.[33]

Cornish pixies can metamorphose into goats, so as to be able to steal away the best milkers from human flocks – and William Bottrell at one point uses the word *bucca* as an alternative for goat. The shapeshifting power may also be used to scare wayward humans. In William Bottrell's story of *Uter Bosence and the Piskey,* the man is drunkenly making his way home on foot from St Just towards Trannack Hill near Sancreed. At Bosence, a fog arose and he became piskey-laden, unable to find the gate out of a field and with the hedges growing taller around him. To this point, the story is typical of the pixie-led pranks that shall be examined at the end of the book. In this case, however, Uter decided to rest at the ruined chapel that still stands near to Bosence farm and to smoke his pipe until the weather improved or dawn came. Instead, though, he was confronted with a band of spriggans and a terrible goat-like being with blazing eyes and paws instead of hooves, which tried to dance with him. Uter struck the piskey-goat to keep it away and was in turn knocked over and then dragged across the moor

---

33 Hunt, *Popular Romances*, 96; R. King, 'Folklore of Devonshire,' *Fraser's Magazine*, vol.8, 1873, 781.

APPEARANCE

– an experience from which he never fully recovered.[34]

The Cornish pixies can also transform themselves into a variety of small birds such as redbreasts, yellowhammers and wag-tails. For example, in the story of *The Fairy Dwelling on Silena Moor* we learn that pixie abductee Grace Hutchens is more reconciled to her captivity by the fact that she can transform into a small bird and fly near to her former lover, Mr Noy. There's a catch to the Cornish pixies' ability to metamorphose, though. It seems each transformation shrinks them, so that eventually they dwindle away to virtually nothing, becoming no bigger than an ant.[35]

The shape-shifting so far has been into the form of animals or objects. An unusual account from Dartmoor in 1876 reported that the pixies were sometimes to be seen as white spots of light moving about in the dark. They could be heard then, too, although nobody has yet understood the words used.[36]

---

34 Bottrell, *Hearthside Tales*, vol.2, 189 and 1, 57.
35 Wentz, *Fairy Faith*, 176.
36 *Transactions of Devonshire Association*, vol.8, 1876, 57.

CHAPTER THREE

Character

Pixies seem to have an especially bad reputation: they may sometimes be good, kind and caring, but they are more frequently mischievous and harm those they dislike. It is occasionally suggested that the Cornish pixies are worse tempered than the Dartmoor ones, but this may be a matter of county rivalry as much as fact. The pixies' mischief (or playfulness, if we're being generous about it) is ingrained in their natures, so much so that it's even been said that their king deliberately sends his subjects on errands to torment and trick us humans. These pranks notwithstanding, the overall assessment seems to be positive: they have been described as "happy and sportive" and "frolicsome."[37]

Against the negative impressions, we might set the common Cornish expression "to laugh like a piskie" which, on the face of it, implies a cheery character. However, we should also note William Bottrell's reference, in his story of piskey-led Uter Bosence, to "mocking laughter

---

37 A. Bray, *Description of the Part of Devonshire Bordering on the Tamar and Tavy* (London, Grant and Griffith, 1836), 173–4; W. Wright, Picturesque South Devonshire, 16; Bowring, 'Devonshire Pixies,' *Once a Week Magazine*, vol.16, Jan.-June 1867, 204; M. E. Whitcomb, *Bygone Days in Devon and Cornwall*, 1874, 45.

as nothing but a piskey ever made." With the pixies, the joke is generally on you, rather than being shared.[38]

As we shall discuss later in chapter eight, a perpetual source of entertainment (to the pixies) and of annoyance and peril (to us) is their habit of leading us astray at night. People might be pixy-led on Exmoor in revenge for some perceived offence (which might be as little as seeing the pixies by chance) or they might make the fog come down on Dartmoor just to laugh at the effect on travellers. Fortunately, the ways to dispel their enchantment are usually quite simple.[39]

Privacy

Robert Hunt described the pixies as both a nuisance and unsociable. They are frequently said to be solitary creatures, by which is meant that they avoid humans – only appearing at twilight and preferring out-of-the-way hills, streams and woods – rather than implying that they don't like the company of their own kind. The general opinion is that the pixies are a sociable people, but that they are jealous of their privacy and don't like to be the subject of human curiosity (although they themselves are endlessly and shamelessly curious about human affairs). It is only those people endowed by long descent with pixy-sight, or those who are favoured by the pixie folk themselves, who are ever likely to see them – and,

---

38 C. Berry, *Cornwall*, 1949, 206; Bottrell, *Traditions and Hearthside Stories*, vol.1,56.
39 Snell, *Exmoor*, 255; Tozer, *Devonshire*, 76 and 81; Northcote, 'Devonshire Folklore,' *Folklore*, vol.11, 1900, 212

even then, it may only be a fleeting glimpse as they flee to shelter.[40]

That said, in the mid-twentieth century a woman was assaulted by a pixie when she was sitting quietly in the woods near Berry Pomeroy castle in Devon. He ran along the log where she had seated herself, slapped her face, and then vanished. Presumably his outrage at her presence in what he considered to be his private domain was so great that revealing himself seemed less important than expressing his displeasure.[41]

Breaches of pixie privacy – and their con-sequences – are central to several stories told in Cornwall about girls employed to work for the *pobel vean* as nurses and house maids. The most famous of these concerns Cherry of Zennor, but several closely related accounts exist, such as those of Grace and Robin or 'Bob o' the Carn,' of Jenny Permuen of Towednack and, thirdly, a tale told to Evans Wentz by a Penzance architect regarding another Zennor girl who went to work for a gentleman who lived at Zimmerman Cottage, The Coombe in Newlyn (an address that still exists). In all these cases the girl is told not to enter certain rooms in the house where she lives and works and not to touch herself with certain ointment. She breaks these injunctions and acquires pixy-sight, meaning that she discovers the truth about her employer's actual nature. As a result, she is promptly expelled from the household.[42]

---

[40] Bowring, 'Devonshire Pixies,' *Once a Week Magazine*, vol.16, Jan.-June 1867, 204; F. Mathews, *Tales of the Blackdown Borderland*, 1923, 55 and 56; Page, *An Exploration of Dartmoor*, 38.
[41] M. Johnson, *Seeing Fairies*, 43.
[42] Hunt, *Popular Romances*, vol.1, 110 and 120; Bottrell, *Traditions and Hearthside Stories*, vol.2, 173; Wentz, *Fairy Faith* 175; .

CHARACTER

These last stories concern people who act deliberately against the pixies' instructions. The little folk can be just as upset by those who unintentionally or inadvertently discover or disturb them. A woman who lived near Minehead in North Somerset accidentally saw twenty-four pixies at Great Gate on Exmoor. In revenge, they led her all night over the moor and through woods. A Mr Tresillian was returning from Penzance to Porthleven when he came upon the pixies dancing in rings. He may have been a little drunk, because he got off his horse with the intention of joining in. The pixies' response was to swarm over him like bees so that he felt as though he was being attacked with needles and pins. He turned his glove inside out and threw it at his assailants, which caused them to vanish.[43]

The pixies' secretive nature seems to extend to their belongings as well. For instance, a man digging peat on Dartmoor during the early 1960s uncovered a small bowl. He put it to one side and carried on with his work and, when he came to look for it when he paused for his lunch, discovered that it had disappeared.[44]

One Cornishman who crossed a faery ring without first turning his pockets inside out as protection experienced a curious punishment. The pixies caught him, pinched him, bound his limbs with threads of gossamer and then touched his eyes with their green ointment. This meant he could see the feasting and revelry going on around him, but was powerless to join in – or to escape. Here,

---

Briggs, *Dictionary of Fairies*, under 'Fairy Widower.'
[43] F. Hancock, *Parish of Selworthy*, 1877, 248; Snell, *Book of Exmoor*, 254; Hunt, *Popular Romances*, 'St Leavan Fairies.'
[44] St Leger Gordon, *Witchcraft and Folklore*, 20.

the pixies violated their own secrecy with the aim of taunting, even of torturing, their victim.[45]

A breach of the pixies' right to privacy is seen as a serious act of disrespect, and they will always quickly take steps to punish it, as with many other acts by humans that they feel show a want of consideration or deference.

Respect

The pixies don't like doubters.[46] In the Dartmoor story of Nanny Norrish, her scepticism was answered one night when she met the pixies piled up before her in a pyramid and all chattering loudly. Nanny appears to have got off lightly, as another writer averred that the pixies' "malevolence will know no end" towards one who's spoken ill of them.[47]

This statement may be affirmed by the case of a miner called Tom Trevorrow, who doubted the existence of the knockers in mines. He refused to share his food with them and ignored the warnings of their displeasure at his disrespect (falls of stones in the workings), so finally they caused a roof collapse that buried the lode he had been working, along with all his tools. Likewise, a man called Barker from Towednack hatched a reckless plan to steal the knockers' tools and was lamed for his presumption. A third miner, named Trenwith, promised the knockers a share of his profits if they guided him to a rich vein. They helped and he became rich, but he didn't keep his side

---

[45] Harris *Cornish Saints and Sinners* c.19.
[46] G. Herbert, 'Devonian Folklore Illustrated,' *Devonshire Association for the Advancement of Science, Literature and Art*, vol.2, 1867, 79.
[47] Crossing *Tales of Dartmoor Pixies* c.7; Page, *Dartmoor* 37.

of the bargain, which led to a curse on his descendants.[48]

Transactions with the pixies must always be honoured. Comparable to this last account is the Devonshire story of a farmer from near Exmouth. He was always kind and respectful to the local pixies and in return they made sure his farm prospered. He laid out an annual feast for them, on the understanding that no-one would spy on them whilst they enjoyed it. In time, the man died and his sons took over the holding. They continued the tradition, but they also appointed a new servant who chose to disobey their instructions by trying to see the pixies feasting. His presence was detected and the pixies vanished. From that day onwards, the farm struggled: the milk soured, the butter wouldn't come in the churn, cheese wouldn't set, the apple crop failed, cattle died in the fields and the grain was blighted.[49]

Later, in chapter six, I'll discuss the pixies' habit of using our homes at night and how they require us to make them welcome. If we fail to prepare adequately, we can again expect the worst. A couple of Dartmoor servant girls were expected, by the family they worked for, to put out water for the pixies before they went to bed at night. One night they forgot and the pixies made a nuisance downstairs. One of the pair refused to get up to correct the mistake and she was lamed for seven years in revenge, whilst the one who did make the effort found silver pennies in the empty water pail in the morning.[50]

In the introduction I mentioned St Nun's Well at Pelynt, also called the Piskies' Well, at which bent pins

---

48 Deane and Shaw, *Folklore of Cornwall*, 69.
49 'Devonshire Pixies,' *Trewman's Exeter Flying Post*, Aug.18th 1869, 6.
50 Bray, *Description*, 188.

were offered to the pixies by throwing them into the stone basin of the spring. A local farmer very unwisely decided that he could use the basin as a trough in his pigsty and he took his team of oxen there to drag it away. After much heaving the basin finally came loose and was then hauled laboriously up a slope until, near the top, the chains broke and the stone rolled all the way back to its original position. The oxen then dropped dead on the spot and the farmer appeared to have a stroke, becoming lame and losing the power of speech.[51]

Religion

The pixies are said to avoid churches, possibly because they are the spirits of the unbaptised (as described earlier in chapter one). One writer declared, quite definitively, that the Devonshire pixies had neither religious services nor rites; confounding this, we have Robert Hunt's statement that the small people, or spriggans (we might also say knockers) would assemble in mines for midnight mass on Christmas Eve.[52]

An aversion to the Christian faith was certainly manifest at Portland, Cadbury and Withycombe in Dorset, where the church bells drove off the local pixies. The pixies residing on a farm at Withypool on Exmoor also had to retreat to the other side of Winsford Hill, a distance of around four to five miles, to escape the sound of the 'ding-dongs.' At Ottery St Mary, south Devon, in

---

51 Quiller-Couch, M and L, *Ancient and Holy Wells of Cornwall*, 1894, 175.
52 Elias Tozer, *Devonshire and Other Original Poems*, 1873, 76; Bowring, 'Devonshire Pixies,' *Once a Week Magazine*, vol.16, Jan.-June 1867, 205; Hunt, *Popular Romances*, vol.2, 123.

1454, the pixies objected to some bells being installed in the newly built church in the town. They tried to abduct the bell-ringers and, when that plan failed, fled for shelter to the nearby Pixies Parlour which Coleridge described in his 1793 poem, *Song of the Pixies*.[53]

If the pixies aren't Christians, what do they believe? In William Bottrell's story of *The House on Silena Moor,* faery abductee Grace makes this remarkable statement about her pixie captors: "'they are not of our religion,' said she, in answer to his surprised look, but star-worshippers.'" If the Silena Moor account truly represents Cornish pixie belief of the late nineteenth century, it might be a relic of the older conception of the pixies' origins as ancient British pagans, perhaps worshipping at the county's many ancient monuments. It's fascinating to learn that the fairy king, Gwyn ap Nudd was said in the Welsh Triads to have great knowledge about the nature and qualities of the stars and could predict the future from them. Gwyn is mainly associated with Wales, but he is also said to have a palace beneath the Tor at Glastonbury, in north-east Somerset. Perhaps, therefore, this knowledge of the stars lingered amongst the *pobel vean*.

Offerings

Regular offerings of small objects were once considered highly advisable so as to keep on the right side of the little folk. The Dartmoor pixies always appreciate a gift of pins, some ribbon or even just a bundle of grass left at the Pixies' Cave on Sheepstor and will reward the donor. Pins may also be left at Pixy Holt on the moor. At Newlyn,

---
53 Tongue, *Somerset Folklore*, 117.

in the west of Cornwall, the *bucca* was given fish daily by fishermen to help ensure a good catch on the next fishing trip.[54] These are general marks of veneration, but the offerings can have more specific motives. One Dartmoor sheep farmer's flock was plagued by disease; he concluded that the only remedy was to go to the top of a tor and slaughter a sheep for the pixies – a move which promptly alleviated the problem.[55]

---

54 Coxhead, *Devon Traditions*, 50; 'Pixies of Devonshire,' *Newcastle Courant*, Dec.25th 1846,3; s. Baring-Gould, *Book of Dartmoor*, 1900, 200; Wentz, *Fairy Faith*, 175.
55 V. C. Clinton-Baddeley, *Dartmoor*, 1925, 97.

CHAPTER FOUR

Places

Pixies are linked to a range of locations, which are distinguished by being isolated and remote, subterranean or ancient, or a combination of these.

Preferring their own company, and wishing to avoid intrusions by humans, the pixies are often said to frequent out-of-the-way upland areas, especially the moors of Somerset, Devon and Cornwall, and deep woodlands. They also frequent the side of streams and rivers and, as a result, these can be amongst the best places to hope to see a pixie.[56]

Ancient Sites

A long barrow at Stoke Courcy in Somerset is known as the Pixies' Mound and another on Beaulieu Heath in Hampshire is called the Pixies Cave. Such ancient sites have been especially associated with the 'spriggans,' who are said to haunt cairns, cromlechs and standing stones – and to be very protective of them.

At Wick in Somerset, there is a pixie mound in a field that's called 'Pixie Piece;' music has been heard coming from the hillock and, if anyone ever tries to dig into it, the soil excavated during the day will be replaced at

---
56   R. Northcote, 'Devonshire Folklore,' *Folklore*, vol.11, 1900, 213.

night. Perhaps not coincidentally, a well with curative powers is found nearby.[57]

Underground Dwellings

Describing Dartmoor, it's been said that "Pixyland is a shadowy realm somewhere beneath the bogs, down which the pixies vanish at the approach of dawn." Like corpses they are hidden beneath the turf; like ghosts they disappear when daylight comes. Mrs Bray stated that the pixies lived inside hollow rocks or in nutshells, emphasising her view of the little folk as truly miniscule.[58]

Numerous locations are named after pixies all over Dartmoor, mainly prominent caves, rocks and tors. For example, at Sheep's Tor it's said that if you enter the cave there and listen you may be able to hear the hum of the pixies' voices and the noise of their work – pounding apples for cider, grinding corn and, on Sundays, the tolling of their church bells. There was a similar location on the other side of the moor near Tavistock specifically called Belfry Rock, Church Rock or the Pixies' Church. Given the pixies' antipathy to church bells seen already, it's puzzling what might have been going on here.[59]

West Country pixies are known to particularly prefer damper ground.[60] On Dartmoor some horses were said to be able to 'smell a pixy,' meaning they could detect the

---

57 Whistler, 'Local Traditions of the Quantocks,' *Folklore*, vol.19, 48.
58 J. Page, *An Exploration of Dartmoor and its Antiquities* (London: Seeley and Co,1892) 37; Bray, *Description*, 177.
59 King, 'Folklore of Devonshire,' *Fraser's Magazine*, vol.8, 1873, 781.
60 Wentz, *Fairy Faith*, 184.

rank, dank smell of the bogs under which they lived.[61] Also on the moor, the bogs where cotton grass grows are said to be the gateways to fairyland, as are quick sands by tidal rivers and clefts and chasms in cliffs and exposed rocks.[62]

In addition, the area around Lustleigh on Dartmoor is a warren of rabbit holes which are believed also to serve as 'pixy holes' – places where the pixies will hide from humans who surprise them when they are too far away from the entrances to escape to their hidden lairs. The preference for underground dwellings seems to apply in Cornwall too, for in 1873 William Bottrell recorded that some small people, about one and a half feet tall, had recently been seen coming out of a hole in the cliffs at Mousehole.[63]

On Dartmoor, there's longstanding animosity between the local foxes and pixies, which has led to an ever-increasing effort by the latter to protect themselves. The foxes hunt the pixies, digging them out of their underground homes and devouring them. The pixies have responded by making iron shelters to protect themselves.[64]

Given the fact that the pixies live under marshy patches, humans have to be careful how they use these areas – even though they may appear to be waste places

---

61 *Transactions of Devonshire Association*, vol.49, 1917, 65.
62 King, 'Folklore of Devonshire,' *Fraser's Magazine*, vol.8, 1873, 781.
63 Bowring, 'Devon Folklore Illustrated,' *Transactions of Devonshire Association for the Advancement of Science, Literature and Art*, vol.2, 1867–8, 78; Bottrell, *Traditions and Hearthside Stories*, vol.2, 245.
64 R. King, 'Folklore of Devonshire,' *Fraser's Magazine*, vol.8, 1873, 781.

of limited agricultural or economic value (to us). In a case from Cornwall, a man turf cutting on Bodmin Moor damaged a 'piskey bed' (an area of bog which was a dancing place) and thereby incurred their wrath. They tried to pixie-lead him with lights at night, but he was too clever for them and always wore a garment inside out. Instead, and rather harmlessly, they resorted to entering his cottage pantry through a keyhole and eating all the biscuits.[65]

Human Habitations

Although Mrs Bray asserted that the pixies prefer the more isolated and wild locations, she contradicted this somewhat with her account of how some pixies near Tavistock loved to spend their nights in an old woman's tulip bed. The flowers apparently thrived from the little folk's beneficial presence. When the elderly woman died this plot was converted by the next residents of the cottage to growing parsley and the aggrieved pixies blighted it.[66]

The relationship with human homes can be even closer than this. For example, in East Cornwall the practice once was to leave holes in the walls of newly built houses so that the pixies' routes weren't blocked; in 1852 a man living at Polyphant near Launceston was asked why he'd allowed his cottage wall to remain in disrepair for years. He said that this was so the pixies could continue to come and go as they always had. Putting up with such apparent

---

65 E. Tregarthen *North Cornwall Fairies and Legends* (London: Wells Gardner, 1906) 115; Wentz, *Fairy Faith*, 184.
66 Bray, *Description*, 190.

discomfort must either be a sign of great respect or of the considerable anxiety that thoughts of pixie displeasure could instil.[67]

Tolerant as the pixies' may be of human dwellings in certain circumstances, and despite the fact that they seem happy to enter them to steal our food and make use of our facilities, it does still depend where they have been constructed. When the building of Fernworthy Hall on Dartmoor disturbed the local pixies, they abducted the family's child in revenge.[68]

---

[67] Courtney, *Cornish Feasts*, 125; *Notes and Queries* 1st series, vol.5, 173.
[68] Coxhead, *Devon Traditions*, 75.

CHAPTER FIVE

Activities

Pixies are most likely to be seen at dusk or dawn,[69] after darkness has fallen [70] and in moonlight – when they dance.[71] Although we shall see some evidence of their industriousness, the pixies will primarily be spotted leading a life of leisure. At Costellas, in Cornwall, for instance, they have been seen sitting in a ring, the men smoking whilst the women spin.[72]

Fairs and Markets

Well-known fairs are held by the Cornish pixies at Pendeen, Breage, Constantine, St Germoe and in Porthleven. In Somerset, fairs are known in several locations with a major market being held at Chard. These gatherings are occasions not just for commerce – selling jewellery, trinkets and sweet snacks – but for general socialisation, with dancing, sports and opportunities for couples to meet.[73]

---

69 Wentz, *Fairy Faith*, 108, 145, 154, 158 and 180.
70 Wentz, 139, 143 and 184.
71 Wentz, 142, 146, 159 and 181.
72 'Pixies of Devonshire,' *Newcastle Courant*, Dec. 25th 1846, 3.
73 Wentz, *Fairy Faith*, 171; Tregarthen, *Folklore Tales*, 'The Pobel Vean Fair,' (1940); Tongue, *Somerset Folklore*, 112; Bottrell, *Traditions and Hearthside Stories*, vol.2, 161.

ACTIVITIES

Anyone who genuinely and honestly deals with the pixies on their terms may expect good treatment if they happen upon one of these events. A man who used to leave out fresh water and cream for the pixies at night went to one of their markets and bought a pewter cider mug. He paid for it in gold and received his change in dry leaves, but wisely did not grumble or question the bargain. He accepted the dead leaves cheerfully and so, the next morning, he found that his mug was silver and his change was lumps of gold. In a related incident, a man came across a pixie fair taking place between Pitminster and Blagdon on the Blackdown Hills in Somerset, at which hundreds had gathered. He too bought a mug – and was presented with pebbles as his change. He made no protest at this and was also not surprised to find, when he got home that night, that the mug had changed into a giant puff-ball mushroom. When he awoke the next morning, however, he discovered that the pebbles had become gold.[74]

Another visitor to the same Blackdown fair, a passing farmer from Combe St Nicholas, had nowhere near such a pleasant experience. From a distance, he saw there were numerous stalls: pewterers, pedlars and fruit and ale sellers. He therefore decided to ride amongst the crowds and investigate but, as soon as he got near, he could see no-one – although he felt that he was being crowded and jostled, as if he rode through a throng of people. Coming out the other side, he looked back and saw the fair clearly once again. However, he found himself in pain and hurried on home where "lameness

---
74 F. Mathews, *Tales of the Blackdown Borderland*, 57; Tongue, *Somerset Folklore*, 112.

seized him all on one side" and continued to afflict him for the remainder of his life [75]

Another pixie fair was known at the Gump, near St Just in Penwith. A man walking across this moorland one night heard music and saw the event in progress. The pixies had furze flowers in their hats and there were many gems and marvellously made articles displayed for sale on the stalls. The witness was overcome by greed for the items, so he threw down his hat to try to cover some of the goods and then dashed forward to snatch up whatever he'd caught. Of course, everything disappeared in an instant, and all he found trapped beneath his hat was snails and gossamer threads. William Bottrell tells a related version of such a story, involving an old woman called An' Pee Tregeer. Returning from Penzance market on Halloween, she gets lost on the moor and hears music and sees lights. Following these, she comes upon a fair at which very well-dressed small people, who are no more than two feet high, are bartering and exchanging goods at numerous stalls. She tries to steal some buckles, feels herself jabbed with pins and needles and curses the pixies, who all disappear. They continue to attack her though, until she uses an 'adder charm' (a form of words?) to scare them off.[76]

At human markets, the pixies will attend not to trade but to steal goods using their powers of invisibility. A woman who once spotted them doing so at Minehead was blinded by them; such incidents are very common

---

[75] Keightley, *Fairy Mythology*, 94–5.
[76] J. Blight, *A Week at Land's End*, 1861, 195; Bottrell, *Traditions and Hearthside Stories*, vol.2, 162.

across the south-west, and indeed across the whole of Britain.[77]

Dances, Music and Sports

In 1836 Mrs Bray declared that "of all their amusements, dancing forms their chief delight and this exercise they are always said to practice, like the Druids of old, in a circle or ring." She added that the Dartmoor pixies danced to tunes played by crickets, grasshoppers, frogs, bees and owls.[78]

These celebrations take place in several types of suitable location. Poet and vicar Robert Hawker recorded that the pixies were often heard at Combe, on the North Cornish coast, playing fiddles for dancing and talking. A Zennor girl came upon pixies 'junketting' in an orchard near Newlyn and the Penwith farmer, Mr Noy, who got lost on Silena Moor near St Buryan, also came upon a large group of people in the orchard of a fine house, where they were either dancing or sitting on benches at tables, drinking beer and cider.[79]

Orchards may be kept well mown or closely grazed and so are suitable for social events and dancing. Areas of meadow land seem to be another popular site with the pixies. A highly romanticised account of a dance comes from Chagford on Dartmoor. A man riding home one night saw tiny lights and heard the chiming of tiny bells in a meadow. When he investigated, he found the pixies dancing, some carrying flowers and others resting

---

77 Snell, *Book of Exmoor*, 254.
78 Bray, *Description*, vol.1, 172–173.
79 Hawker, *Footprints of Former Men in Far Cornwall;* Wentz, *Fairy Faith*, 175; Bottrell, *Traditions and Hearthside Stories*, vol.2, 95.

on grass stalks until the first light of dawn drove them home. The pixie preference for meadows is reflected in a rather more sombre account of supernatural activity in a combe near Selworthy on the edge of Exmoor. There the pixies light fires and wash and dress their children at night. What's more, in the same meadow there is a post which none dare to pass in the dark because a shapeless thing with rattling chains will suddenly appear from it and terrify the traveller.[80]

Cornish writer Enys Tregarthen stated that on top of the cliffs at Polzeath there were large rings to be seen, in which the pixies would hold both their dances and their *gammets* (or games). Certainly, the earliest pixie sighting in Cornwall was of a hurling match taking place in a cornfield at Boscastle in August 1657. The game surged back and forth for some time before the supernatural identity of the players was confirmed by their disappearance over a cliff into the sea and by the fact that those watching found afterwards that there was no sign of damage to the crop in the field where the match had taken place. A much later story of a man called Richard Vingoe, who wanders into 'pixie-land' under the cliffs at Land's End, also involves him seeing a pixie game of hurling.[81]

As we might anticipate, anyone who stumbles unwittingly on such fairy revels will be roughly handled. They will be surrounded, tweaked and pulled around the field a dozen times. Then the moon will go behind the

---

[80] S. Hewett, *Nummits and Crummits – Devonshire Customs, Characteristics and Folklore*, 1900, 38; Snell, *Book of Exmoor*, 254; F. Hancock, *Parish of Selworthy*, 1877, 247.
[81] E. Tregarthen, *Pisky Purse*, 1905; Bottrell, *Traditions and Hearthside Stories*, vol.2, 102.

clouds and pixies will vanish, but the trespasser's ordeal will still not be over. They will then follow a light towards their home but instead find themselves pixie-led – until they finally have the presence of mind to turn a pocket or cap.[82]

Pixie Rings

> "If thou'rt of air, let the grey mist fold thee... If a pixie, seek thy ring."[83]

Pixie dances seem to be simple circle dances and one impact of these is to create well marked places where the grass is greener and where mushrooms (or 'pixie-stools') can be seen flourishing the following morning. For example, the Reverend Robert Hawker recorded that the pixie rings on Hennacleeve Hill, near Morwenstow, were one foot wide with darker grass than the rest of the sward. Certain spots are favoured by the pixies for dancing, such as on the cliffs above Newtrain Bay at Trevone near Padstow or at Sea View Green, Trevescan, near Land's End.[84]

These rings can be perilous places. People may be dragged or enticed into the dances and then abducted or their trespass on the rings may offend the pixies and lead to fatal consequences. A 1952 incident has been reported in which a boy on holiday in North Cornwall unwittingly

---

82 Couch, 'Cornish Folklore,' *Penzance Natural History and Antiquarian Society Report*, in *Royal Cornwall Gazette*, Nov.11th, 1853, 6.
83 Sir Walter Scott, *The Pirate*, 1821, 23.
84 Hawker, *Footprints of Former Men in Far Cornwall*; Wentz, *Fairy Faith*, 173, 181 and 182; Tregarthen, *North Cornwall Fairies and Legends*, 171.

played in a fairy ring and, in due course, died as a result. This is an extreme example, but the expectation certainly should be that the hapless human will be pinched viciously and whirled around all night until sunrise. A man walking home drunk near Chudleigh on Dartmoor was caught in a ring near Pixies' Hole and was spun mercilessly around until he fainted with dizziness and exhaustion. He managed to make his way home when he recovered consciousness, but there he took to his bed and died shortly afterwards.[85]

Even if the experience doesn't prove fatal, there is still a risk that the human quitting the dance will find that the world they left has changed. A Mr Maddern of Penzance told Evans Wentz that "time slipped away very, very rapidly, though people returned from the pixies no older than when they went with them." A Zennor girl who worked for a pixie gentleman as nurse to his child found that what had seemed like weeks in his household was actually twenty years on earth; in a very similar story of a servant girl called Grace, what had seemed like less than one year's absence to her was nine years for her family.[86]

Mines

As mentioned at the very start, there is some uncertainty as to the exact nature of the mine fairies. They are frequently called knockers, but whether this implies

---

[85] Deane and Shaw, *Folklore of Cornwall*, 92; Crossing, *Dartmoor Pixies*, c.4; *Reports and Transactions of the Devonshire Association*, vol.8, 1876, 722; HGT, 'Pixies or Pisgies,' *Notes and Queries*, 1850, no.61, 511; Harris *Cornish Saints and Sinners* c.19.
[86] Wentz, *Fairy Faith*, 175; Bottrell, *Traditions and Hearthside Stories*, vol.2, 184.

they are a separate species, or whether they are merely underground pixies, is not clear. In an account of the ordeal of being trapped in a disused mineshaft, a late Victorian writer recorded his fear that his cries for help might have been mistaken for those of a pixie – making clear his belief that knockers and pixies were identical. Some sources even refer to these mine spirits as *buccas* (*bockles* according to Robert Hunt), in which guise they bring luck to miners – so long as food is shared with them.[87]

It's said to be good luck to see the pixies dancing in the adit (or entrance passage) of a mine, for this indicates that there are valuable lodes at this location. The lights seen at night, that are sometimes called 'jack o' lanterns' or wills of the wisp, are in fact the knockers, indicating to those miners whom they favour where it would be most profitable to dig for a good lode of ore.[88]

On Dartmoor, though, the mine pixies may be just as likely to mock and mislead miners with false fires or with the sound of hammer blows. Even so, these hammer blows can be a good sign, leading a man towards a rich seam and stopping when he is in the right place.[89] As a rule, the mine pixies are often heard but very seldom seen. When one Cornish tin miner broke through into a pixie tunnel and discovered a group of knockers at work (whom he said looked like sixpenny dolls, albeit

---

[87] *South Wales Echo*, April 14th 1898, 4 'The Forgotten Mine;' Courtney, *Cornish Feasts and Folklore*, 129; Wentz, *Fairy Faith*, 177; Hunt, *Popular Romances*, vol.1, 79 and 88 and vol.2, 119; Bottrell, *Traditions and Hearthside Stories*, vol.2, 187.
[88] S. Hewett, *Nummits and Crummits*, 50; C. Berry, *Cornwall*, 1949, 206.
[89] Bray, *Description*, 174; 'Cornish Superstitions,' *Weekly Mail*, August 30th 1902, 2.

smoking pipes) they immediately asked him for a candle. Of course, as soon as he looked away to pick one up, they disappeared.[90]

Over and above their insistence upon respect for themselves, and for any bargains made with them, the mine pixies impose a strict moral code upon human miners. They object to whistling and swearing underground and will warn offenders with small falls of rocks.[91]

Livestock

The pixies seem to be very fond of cattle (and of their milk). They are accused, in Devon, of milking cattle dry overnight, so there will be no milk for the farmer in the morning. There also is some suggestion that they may play pranks with cattle, chasing them at night or driving them into the clover (which can cause bloating and sometimes death). Occasionally, the cattle might even be stolen. Rowan crosses hung up in byres, or tied to the cows' tails with red thread, can help avert these threats.[92]

There is a very famous and well-known story of a cow called Rosy which was owned by a farmer at Bosfranken to the west of St Buryan. She produced twice as much milk as the rest of the herd, but had a tendency of wandering off in the evenings. No-one understood this, until Molly the dairy maid was returning from milking Rosy in a field and placed her milk-pail on her head cushioned

---

90 Bottrell, *Traditions and Hearthside Stories*, vol.1 77.
91 J. Hammond, *A Cornish Parish – St Austell*, 1897, 359.
92 Wright, *Picturesque South Devonshire*, 16; Hunt, *Popular Romances*, vol.1, 'The Fairies;' R. Hawker, *Footprints of Former Men in Far Cornwall*; Hunt, *Popular Romances*, vol.1, 66.

by a 'wiese' of grass, which happened to include some four leaved clover. This revealed to her that the pixies were swarming around the cow, drinking milk from her udders but also treating her affectionately. To prevent this theft, the advice from a local 'wise woman' was to rub Rosy's udders with fish brine, as the pixies couldn't abide the smell of fish or the savour of salt or grease. This worked, but the farm also lost all its luck and wealth. A related account, given to Evans Wentz, was that "people of a miserly nature used to put salt around a cow to keep the pixies away." This would prevent them pilfering the milk, but it was said that they would be sure to 'pixy-led' the offending human at the first opportunity.[93]

William Bottrell recorded that wherever goats preferred to graze would be certain to be places frequented by the pixies. In Cornwall, it's believed that the pixies – and especially their babies and changelings – live on goats' milk. Additionally, as mentioned before, any animals that were good-milkers would be enticed away from a human herd by the appearance of mysterious billy-goats, who were actually pixies in disguise.[94]

Whatever their affection for live cattle, the pixies also like to eat them. A story is told of a farmer on Dartmoor who, on two successive mornings, found ash and embers in his hearth and one of his cows reduced to skin and bones. On the third night he resolved to keep watch. Pixies appeared and dragged the cow into the kitchen, where they proceeded to kill, flay and roast it. After their feast, they reassembled the beast, all except for one bone

---

93 Bottrell, *Traditions and Hearthside Stories*, vol.2, 73; Wentz, *Fairy Faith*, 177.
94 Bottrell, *Traditions and Hearthside Stories*, 246.

from its ankle, which was overlooked and which left the resurrected cow with a limp.[95]

Flight

As Mrs Bray described, the pixies "can fly as well as run." Although she was describing Dartmoor, the examples of this ability come from Cornwall.[96]

Some miners had been celebrating Christmas at the pub, after which one of the party, John Sturtridge, started to walk back home to Luxulyan. Part of the way there, he came across some pixies dancing. He tried to hurry on and get away from them, but they set about pixie-leading him so that he was trapped and going in circles, with their laughter ringing in his ears. Then he suddenly heard a chorus of tiny voices shout, "Ho! and away for Par Beach!" Wanting to escape his predicament, John repeated the shout, and was in an instant at Par. The pixies had a brief dance and then one of them cried "Ho! and away for Squire Tremain's cellar!" John repeated what he heard and was straightaway in the cellars at Heligan, enjoying the owner's beer and wine. John drank rather too much, on top of what he'd already consumed, and was found asleep the next morning by the butler. No-one believed his impossible story; he was arrested, tried for theft and sentenced to death. On the day of his execution a pixie woman appeared before the scaffold and shouted "Ho! and away for France!" John repeated the words – and escaped his doom.[97]

---

95 J. Coxhead, *Devon Traditions and Fairy Tales*, 51.
96 Bray, *Peeps at Pixies*, 11.
97 Hunt, *Popular Tales*, 76.

ACTIVITIES

A very similar journey was made by a boy returning at night from Polperro to Porthallow on the Helford River. He heard a voice declare, "I'm for Porthallow Green" and repeated the words. He flew there in an instant. Then the voice said, "I'm for Seaton Beach" (near Polperro) and flew there in a flash. Next was the King of France's cellar, where he ate, drank and pocketed a golden goblet, which he produced as proof of his unbelievable adventures when he got home.[98]

---

98 J. Couch, *History of Polperro*, 135.

CHAPTER SIX

Human Relations

Pixies interact with the human population around them in a variety of ways. Some of these can be malign, as the next chapter will describe, but some can be co-operative and tolerant, if not exactly friendly. Indeed, on Exmoor there are said to be 'pixie-men' who have very good connections with the local little folk and are able to work with them harmoniously and profitably.[99]

We should note a brief observation by Enys Tregarthen that there was a belief around St Columb in North Cornwall that the pixies would pass over your nose whilst you slept and would order your dreams. The Devonshire pixies were reported to bring nightmares to some and sweet dreams to others whilst another writer has said that the Cornish pixies will tickle your nose to awaken you when you're having a bad dream. These are rather scattered and inconclusive references, but the fairy link to dreams is not an entirely isolated idea in British folklore, if we recall the powers of Queen Mab as reputed midwife of dreams.[100]

---
99 Snell, *Book of Exmoor*, 256.
100 Tregarthen, *North Cornwall Fairies and Legends,* 110; Bowring, 'Devonshire Pixies,' *Once a Week Magazine,* vol.16, Jan.-June 1867, 206; Harris, *Cornish Saints and Sinners,* c.19; on Mab, see my *Famous Fairies,* 2020.

Gold

All faery folk tend to be associated with possessing, or knowing the whereabouts of, buried treasure. In Cornwall, this is an attribute especially of the spriggans, who are said jealously and violently to protect their gold. In one case at Trencrom Hill they conjured up a storm and *en masse* attacked a thief who was digging for a rumoured crock of gold.[101]

In the far west of Cornwall, in Penwith, the belief was that quantities of gold are buried around ancient monuments, quoits, barrows and rounds, and that these can be discovered with the help of a captive spriggan, knocker or pixie. The prospective treasure hunter has to be agile, though, to be able to capture the pixie and the person must also be quick to ask his questions before the pixie vanishes or shrinks to the size of an ant. It's also said in Cornwall that if tin is placed in an ant's nest at the time of a new moon, the pixies will voluntarily transmute it into silver for you.[102]

Cornish fairy writer Enys Tregarthen, in her 1911 story *Hunting Fairies*, indicated that a human will never find pixie gold by deliberately searching for it. Having failed to locate treasure by watching for pixies digging, her character Carveth throws away his pick axe carelessly. He is then told to dig wherever it happened to fall – and by this means he finds a crock of coins. In another of her stories, Tregarthen related how two children who used to watch the pixies dancing in their rings above Polzeath

---
101 Bottrell, *Traditions and Hearthside Stories*, vol.2, 245.
102 Bottrell, *Traditions and Hearthside Stories*, vol.1, 74; Courtney, *Cornish Feasts*, 125.

Bay, hearing their laughter and seeing their lights, would from time to time find 'piskey purses' on the beach, which contained gold. An odd story from Wendron, near Marazion, tells of a woman who was visited one night by two pixies, who voluntarily told her that a vast treasure lay buried beneath her cottage. Forty years later, in 1906, newspapers reported that her grandson was excavating a shaft beneath where her home had stood in the hope of locating this hoard. [103]

Gold may be won from the pixies by magical means, but it's inevitable that some people will try to steal it. The Gump near St Just has long been known as a place frequented by the *pobel vean* and the pixies who gather there have been reported to have given small but valuable presents to those they have favoured and allowed to see them. Of course, anyone who trespasses uninvited or who tries to take what isn't theirs runs a considerable risk. A greedy old man living in St Just resolved to try to steal some of the pixie treasure during one of their moonlit feasts. One night, he hid himself near the Gump and waited for a chance to seize some gold. The hill opened and a host of spriggans emerged in a blaze of light and seemed to surround the old man. Then a magnificent feast with many guests began. The miser saw a chance to steal one of the fine cups or platters but, as he began to creep forward, he realised that the spriggans had thrown ropes around him. He was quickly pinned down and could not move, even though it felt as if a swarm of bees was stinging him. The pixies disappeared at dawn, when the old man came to his senses, and found himself tied to

---

103 E. Tregarthen, *Folklore Tales*, 2020; *Pisky Purse*, 1905. 'Treasure Hunt in Cornwall,' *Cardiff Times*, August 25th 1906, 2.

the ground by gossamer webs. He went home, cold, wet, ashamed – and empty handed.[104]

Pixie gold can also take the form of coins but, needless to say, obtaining the pixie money by theft or trickery is still a very bad idea. There is a story of a fisherman from Polperro who discovered a group of pixies on the village beach, counting out money and sharing it between them. The man slipped his hat in amongst those of the *pobel vean* and got some coins allocated to him. He then tried to make off with the money he had tricked out of them, but the enraged pixies chased the thief all the way home.[105]

A related story comes from further west. An old widow living at Chy-an-wheal, above Carbis Bay, found that her home was favoured by the thievish spriggans of nearby Trencrom Hill. They resorted to her cottage to divide up their plunder and rewarded her tolerance of this by leaving her a coin after each visit. She hatched a plan to get more from them and, one night, secretly turned her shift inside out whilst the spriggans were present. This enabled her to seize a gold cup from them. The widow became a wealthy woman as a result, but she could never wear that shift again because, if she did, she suffered agonies.[106]

All the foregoing paragraphs suggest that the pixies have no objection to metals (as does their presence in mines). However, other evidence contradicts this. As we shall see later in chapter seven, the pixies dislike iron implements. In West Cornwall knobs of lead called 'pixie

---

104 Hunt, *Popular Romances*, 88.
105 J. Couch, *History of Polperro*, 137.
106 Hunt, *Popular Tales*, 113.

feet' were put on the ridge tiles of farmhouse roofs to prevent the pixies dancing up there and to stop them souring the milk in the dairy. Perhaps the pixies dislike base metals as opposed to precious metals. Then again, they can be contrary: another folklorist reported that around Helston these lead 'pixy-pots' actually encouraged pixie dancing and were considered to bring the house good luck.[107]

Household Visitors

"Pelm in ahind the door/ Pail o' water on the floor" is the Somerset advice on how to prepare for the arrival of pixie visitors at night in your home. 'Pelm' is dust, meaning that the house should be tidied (after a fashion). Readers may recall that, at the close of Shakespeare's *Midsummer Night's Dream,* Puck is "sent with broom before/To sweep the dust behind the door." He spruces up the palace in advance of the arrival of Oberon and Titania; in fact, across Britain, fairies insisted on homes being cleaned before they entered them.[108]

These kinds of preparation apply on Dartmoor too: basins of water should be left out near the fire, in response to which small sums of money may be left for the householder (but only so long as this generosity isn't gossiped or boasted about to friends and neighbours). If water isn't left out, the pixies will upset the sauce pans and sour the milk. What has to be understood is that

---

107 Courtney, *Cornish Feasts* 126; Deane and Shaw *Folklore of Cornwall* 91. Of course, the faeries can be contrary: S. Baring-Gould, *A Book of Cornwall*, 1899, c.XVI.
108 *Midsummer Night's Dream*, Act 5, scene 2.

pixies certainly can't be excluded from your home – so it is plainly only sensible to accommodate them. They are a very curious people and they can get in through keyholes and cracks; no locks or bolts will keep them out. Once inside a house, they can get into cupboards and cabinets at will and will pilfer food such as butter, junkets and sweet cakes.[109]

In Cornwall, it was thought wise to leave out food and to build up a good fire on stormy nights so that the pixies would have somewhere warm and welcoming to take shelter. This is, of course, pure pragmatism; they'll be coming anyway so you might as well do your best to make them feel comfortable. This could be to your benefit; not to do so will make you sorry.[110]

Household Help

The good news is that the pixies won't just take their ease in your home; they may come inside in order to undertake household tasks for you. However, they must *never* be watched when doing this work and, if they are, they will never visit the house again.[111]

On Exmoor bread and milk as well as water and towels are left out for the pixies, who in return will perform domestic chores for residents, such as cleaning the house, completing unfinished brewing, washing dishes and clothes, completing knitting, sharpening knives, leavening loaves and sweetening or strengthening cider.

---

[109] Tongue, *Somerset Folklore*, 118,' Bray, *Description*, 156 and 174–175; Crossing, *Tales of Dartmoor Pixies*, c.3.
[110] Wentz, *Fairy Faith*, 171 and 182.
[111] Tregarthen, *North Cornwall Fairies and Legends*, 167 or *Folklore Tales*, 'Curious Woman of Davidstow,' (1940).

Amongst the tasks performed by the Devonshire pixies is the spinning of the occupiers' flax for them. In Cornwall, they spin with cotton-rush, which is termed 'pisky wool.' There's an intriguing report from 1962 of meals being prepared for some holiday visitors staying in a Dartmoor cottage.[112]

There are a couple of accounts from Dartmoor of coins being left out for the pixies at night so that they will sweep the kitchen, churn the butter and perform other tasks. Usually, it has to be observed, paying for the work to be done by the little people is not how this relationship functions and to attempt to commercialise what they see as a voluntary boon will virtually always prove to be a bad idea. The pixies can also bestow more long-term benefits upon favoured individuals, but they must again be treated with the usual discretion and respect. It was recorded in 1827 that a house in Topsham in Devon was blessed with a pixie barrel of beer, which never ran dry. Sadly, one day, a maid servant pulled out the bung and peered inside – and the barrel lost its magical bounty.[113]

In Cornwall, there is a truly domesticated pixie, acting to all intents and purposes exactly like a northern English brownie, and attached to a particular family or house. These 'brown pixies' will happily undertake a range of

---

[112] Snell, *Book of Exmoor*, 254; Kingsley Palmer, *Folklore of Somerset*, 1976, 22; Bowring, 'Devonshire Pixies,' *Once a Week Magazine*, vol.16, Jan.-June 1867, 206; *Reports and Transactions of the Devonshire Association*, vol.8, 1876, 57; R. Northcote, 'Pixies in the Present Day,' *Devon Notes and Queries*, (1901), vol.1, no.20, 38; Bray, *Description*, 175; R. Hawker, *Footprints of Former Men in Far Cornwall*, 1893; K. Briggs, *The Fairies in Tradition and Literature*, 164–5.

[113] Crossing *Tales of Dartmoor Pixies* c.3 and 4; V. C. Clinton-Baddeley, *Devon*, 102.

household chores and cleaning, just so long as they are not watched by the occupants. One used to appear over a period of months in a farmhouse kitchen at Werrington, near Launceston, in the form of a small child. It was treated very much as a member of the household, being given its own stool to sit upon, and it did a great deal of house work. If the chimney and hearth had not been swept, it would pinch the maid. Another was to be found at Killigarth manor in Cornwall. There it supervised the cooking in the kitchen, watching the roast on the spit over the fire and getting a servant to remove it when it was cooked.[114]

An old Cornish mill also had a pixie attached to it, who used to do the grinding for customers. As well as his manual labours, he had a keen moral sense. He always gave full measure to people, unlike the miller himself, and the pixie would often tickle the miller's palm to remind him he was cheating. One day, there was an error in a delivery and an argument developed between the miller and his wife. To begin with he blamed her, then the man blamed the pixie. For this wrongful accusation, the pixie swore not to do another stroke of work in the mill for the next two generations.[115]

There is some evidence to suggest that the pixies' interests and powers extend well beyond the basic domestic economy to much more fundamental issues. In late 1971 *Countryman* magazine featured a letter that described how pixies had restored and maintained the water levels in the well of a remote Cornish cottage, all in

---

[114] *Notes and Queries*, 1st series, vol.2 (1850), 475; Couch, 'Cornish Folklore,' *Penzance Natural History and Antiquarian Society Report*, in *Royal Cornwall Gazette*, Nov.11th, 1853, 6.
[115] Harris, *Cornish Saints and Sinners*, c.19.

return for the corners of Cornish pasties, broken off and laid around the well head on the night of a new moon. Unfortunately, when the owner went away and left the property in the hands of caretakers, they failed to keep up the offerings and the well dried up again. Perhaps this concern for the wider viability and prosperity of a small holding connects with the pixies' friendliness towards livestock, their control over the weather (see later in chapter seven) and the idea that they can bring (or remove) a farm's luck.[116]

Harvest and Threshing

The pixies can be quite involved in the whole human enterprise of growing and processing of crops. At the very least, they should be appeased at harvest time by those working in the fields sharing with them a little of their food and drink; on Exmoor it was even said that a good meal laid out in the fields at night would persuade the pixies to reap your corn for you – and to do a good job of it too. This belief has to be contrasted to the experience of one Dartmoor farmer, who found that his harvested sheaves had been disarranged overnight. He sorted out the mess in his field and then decided to watch what was happening the next night. Sure enough, pixies appeared and pulled all the sheaves into one corner of the field. One of the little people complained how sweaty he was getting doing this, which triggered an angry intervention from the man – and, of course, his unwanted helpers all vanished.[117]

---

116 Janet Bord, *Fairies*, 18.
117 Courtney, *Cornish Feasts and Folklore*, 129; Snell, *Book of*

The pixies will enter barns and help with threshing, displaying great skill and energy, but, as is the case across the British Isles, if they are spied upon, or given clothing in recognition of their labours, they will depart for ever, often with the parting words:

> "Pixie fine, pixie gay
> Pixie now will fly away," or

> "Pixie has new coat,
> Pixie has new hood;
> Pixie will never now do more good."

The pixie threshers can also be repelled by merely verbal thanks. A Somerset farmer found them energetically threshing his grain and expressed his gratitude for their labours. They never helped him again – being seen *and* thanked was too much. A gift of food is, however, acceptable – as just seen on Exmoor. Why clothes should be insulting but a meal is not can't easily be explained, especially as, in at least one case, the naked pixie doing the threshing was heard to sing, "Little Pixy, fair and slim, without a rag to cover him." Any farmer overhearing such a song would surely be forgiven for taking this to be a lament and for thinking that having a small suit made was an act of welcome charity.[118]

In fact, it seems that it is all too easy to scare the pixies away from their labours. In a Cornish story, an old

---

Exmoor, 256; Crossing, *Dartmoor Pixies*, c.8.
118 Deane and Shaw, *Folklore of Cornwall*, 91; Crossing, *Dartmoor Pixies*, c.6; J. Couch, *History of Polperro*, 136; Wentz, *Fairy Faith*, 172; Tongue, *Somerset Folklore*, 117–118; HGT, 'Pixies or Pisgies,' *Notes and Queries*, 1850, no.61, 514; Bottrell, *Traditions and Hearthside Stories*, vol.2, 168.

woman walking home at night comes across a crowd of them threshing in a barn. She watches them for a while until one sneezes; instinctively, she says 'Bless you!' at which the pixies vanish.[119]

A Devonshire farmer called Robin faced an opposite problem. He found that his threshing never seemed to reduce the pile of unhusked grain in his barn. He watched one night and discovered that the pixies were actually bringing their own wheat into his barn. Enraged, he chased them off and was able then to finish his work, but they had their revenge by appearing to him as a very bright light when he was out poaching one night – terrifying him by making him think he'd been caught.[120]

Other farm tasks may also be undertaken, albeit by rather more magical means. On Dartmoor the pixies were said to assist farmers by helping ewes to have two lambs or filling cow's udders. They would also deliver loads of hay or straw for lucky smallholders.[121]

At harvest time, an orchard should never be cleared of fruit completely. A few apples must always be left behind for the pixies – an offering which is called the 'pixy-word' (or hoard). If this is done, they will bless the next year's crop. Somerset pixies are believed to love apple trees and orchards above all places.[122]

A last story, from the north of Dartmoor, connects us with an issue to be considered very shortly. A farmer caught the pixies threshing corn in his barn. They fled

---

[119] Bottrell, *Traditions and Hearthside Stories*, vol.2, 154.
[120] Northcote, 'Devonshire Folklore,' 214.
[121] Bowring, 'Devonshire Pixies,' *Once a Week Magazine*, vol.16, Jan.-June 1867, 206; R. Northcote, 'Pixies in the Present Day,' *Devon Notes and Queries*, (1901), vol.1, no.20, 38.
[122] Dathen *Somerset Fairies and Pixies* 15, 28 and 114; Mathews, *Blackdown Borderland*, 55; Tongue, *Somerset Folklore* 119.

when he appeared and all escaped except one, whom he snatched up and put in his lantern. The pixie lived in there for some time until one night the man left the door of the lantern open and then his captive was able to make off, crying "Here I goes, here I goes."[123]

Repairs

Just as the pixies may undertake chores for humans, the reverse can occur. A common theme across Britain is the rewarding of a human who does a good deed for the pixies by repairing some tool for them. In one very typical example, a Somerset farmer mended a broken peel (a baking implement) for the pixies and was given a freshly baked loaf – and good luck for life – in return. A similar Devon story involved two men. One repaired a broken peel and, in thanks, the pixies left cider for them both. The man's companion refused to drink this – and was pinched in punishment. A curious reversal of this theme also comes from the same county. A story set on Dartmoor tells how a hungry ploughman working in a field heard the pixies call out – "the oven's hot." He cheerfully responded, "bake me a cake then," and was indeed rewarded with a freshly made treat. As important as good deeds is a preparedness to accept whatever gift the pixies then make to you.[124]

If mending pixie tools is rewarded, maliciously damaging them will inevitably attract the little folk's vengeance. A boy found a fairy peel in a field and deliberately broke it, crying out in glee "the pixies won't

---
123 Bowring, 'Devon Folklore,' 77.
124 Tongue, *Somerset Folklore*, 116; Crossing, *Dartmoor Pixies*, c.7.

bake any bread anymore." For his wilful act of destruction, he was pinched so severely that he couldn't open his eyes for days.[125]

Related to mending chattels may be the act of giving aid to the pixies themselves, whether they are ill or experiencing childbirth. In one Somerset tale the human nurse refused any payment for tending a sick pixie woman and stayed caring for the invalid as long as she was required. For this devotion to duty, she was rewarded with hens that laid better than before and more generous gifts from her subsequent human patients.[126]

Catching

Elusive as they are, pixies are captured from time to time. Speed and surprise are predictably essential to catching a magical creature – in one story from Dartmoor it's only an incredibly lucky jab with a fork that pins a pixie to a stool and prevents his escape from a house.[127]

The story of *Skillywidden* concerns a pixie boy captured at Treridge near Zennor. A farmer was cutting furze when he spotted a young pixie (or spriggan) asleep. He scooped the boy up and took him home where he was named Bobby Griglans by the human family. He seems to have coped well with his situation and would play contentedly by the hearth with the children. The pixie child promised to reveal to the farmer where gold was buried on a nearby hill, just as soon as the nights were moonlit. However, one day when the youngsters had all slipped outside to play, the pixie's parents came

---

125 Northcote, 'Devonshire Folklore,' 213.
126 Mathews, *Tales of the Blackdown Borderland*, 59.
127 Crossing, *Dartmoor Pixies*, c.9– 'The Pixies' Revel.'

searching for him and he readily went home with them. The farmer spanked his children for their carelessness and never got his hidden gold. Readers may like to note that there is a farm called Skillywadden to the south of Trendrine Hill where this incident took place; this may therefore be prime pixie catching country, although we ought also to note that Cornish writer Enys Tregarthen used 'skilly whidden' as a general term to denote a pixie child.[128]

In another incident, two pixies were accidentally caught by poachers who trapped them in sacks, believing them to be rabbits. As the men carried their haul home, they heard voices from inside the sacks, discussing their predicament. The pair were so scared by this that they dropped their burdens and ran off, allowing the pixies to escape.[129]

In the instances cited so far, the captured pixies had to wait either to be rescued or for an opportunity to make their getaway to come. Given their magical powers, we might anticipate that it really ought to be very easy indeed for a pixie to escape any type of confinement. This was definitely the experience of a Dartmoor woman returning from market, who came across a pixy about eighteen inches tall. She snatched him up and shut him in her shopping basket. After some initial complaining (in a "strange jargon" that sounded to her like "gibberish") the pixy fell silent and, on opening the lid to check on the little creature, she found that he'd disappeared.[130]

---

[128] Bottrell, *Traditions*, vol.1, 74; Tregarthen, *Folklore Tales*, 'Skerry Werry' and 'The Nurse Who Broke Her Promise,' (1940).
[129] Bowring, 'Devon Folklore,' 78.
[130] Crossing *Tales of Dartmoor Pixies* c.5.

A south Devonshire farmer had a com-parable encounter. As he was walking home from the market at Ottery St Mary, he came across a tiny woman dressed in green in the hedge. He picked her up and took her home with him. His wife advised him to tie the captive to the bedpost overnight but, in the morning, they found only a leek secured there. The man took the leek outside to throw it away when, suddenly, it transformed back into a woman who was met by a host of pixies riding tiny horses.[131]

Sometimes pixies seem to get lost rather than being caught. A farmer of Langreek, near Polperro, was returning home one evening from a distant part of his farm, when, to his surprise, he saw a miserable-looking little human-like creature, sitting on a stone in the middle of a field. He was diminutive in size and apparently very cold and hungry. Pitying the being's condition, and perhaps aware that it was a pixie and that he might be repaid for kind treatment with good luck, the farmer took the child home, where he placed him on a stool by the fire and gave him milk. The poor bantling soon recovered, and, though he never spoke, became very lively and playful. He became a favourite in the family for his amusing tricks and the entire household felt very sorry when their strange guest suddenly deserted them. After three or four days, as the little fellow was gambolling about the kitchen, a shrill voice was heard in the farmyard, calling three times: "Colman Grey!" At this the pixie boy sprang up, cried: "Ho! ho! ho! my daddy is come," flew out through the keyhole, and was never heard of again.[132]

---

[131] 'Devonshire Pixies,' *Trewman's Exeter Flying Post*, Aug.18th 1869, 6.
[132] Couch, *History of Polperro*, 134; *Choice Notes: Folk-Lore*, 73.

Our final example of a lost pixie child involves another farmer from near Ottery St Mary. The man was walking through his fields when he heard a voice crying out that he'd lost his 'Shilo'. The farmer looked over the hedge and saw a little old man, whom he knew straightaway to be a pixie. Soon after, the farmer came across a tiny baby lying near one of his hay ricks and crying feebly. He took the foundling home to his wife, who revived it with bread soaked in warm cider. They realised that the baby must be the missing Shilo for whom the pixie had been searching, so the man returned the infant to the spot where he'd found it. He then called out and quickly the old pixy appeared and carried off the babe, without saying a word to the human. The couple feared they'd face punishment for removing the child, but the next morning they awoke to find their house swept, the fire lit and breakfast already cooked and laid out on the table. Outside, the corn was threshed and the day's farm-work was already done. This continued every day after that and the pair became well off and comfortable.[133]

Pixy Sight

The power to see through glamour, and to see the pixies as they really are, is an ability generally called 'second sight' in Britain, but in the South West it tends to be referred to as 'pixy-sight' or being 'pisky-eyed.'

You may recall the story recounted earlier in chapter one, from the Blackdown Hills of Somerset, in which a woman was brushed across her brow by a large moth

---

133 W. P. Merrick, 'Shilo – A Devonshire Folk Tale,' *Folklore*, vol.22, 1911, 48–49.

and thereby received the 'pixy-sight' which enabled her to see an old pixy man who had come to ask for her skill in nursing his sick wife. We know that fairy powers can be transferred by touch, so this again fits in with wider faerylore, although the medium of the moth is unusual. As is also typical of stories such as these, the privileged sight was taken away again later. Some months after the wife had recovered, the nurse saw her husband at Taunton market and enquired after his spouse's health. He responded by laying his hands on her eyes and blowing, which deprived her of the pixie's gift.[134]

Contact with the pixies seems to be fundamental to the transfer, as is seen in Enys Tregarthen's story of the fairy child *Skerry Werry*. A lost fairy child was taken in and cared for by a widow on Bodmin Moor. The longer the little girl stayed with her, the better the old woman's 'pixy sight' became, so that she found she could see the pisky lights on the moor at night. The story implies that it was simply Skerry-Werry's residence that had the effect. More traditionally, as in Tregarthen's story *The Nurse Who Broke Her Promise*, a human midwife bathing a tiny brown pixie baby is told not to splash bath water in her eyes (or, even more commonly in such tales, is asked to anoint the child with ointment, but not to touch herself) and the breach of the injunction is what transfers the magic vision. The nurse in Tregarthen's story later sees the pixie father stealing at a market and accosts him; once again, he touches her eyes and removes the gift. As this account demonstrates, the pixies seem to have two motives for 'blinding' those that can see them. Firstly, those individuals may have acquired the pixy-sight

---

[134] Mathews, *Tales of the Blackdown Borderland*, 59.

wrongfully (or, at least, no longer require it); secondly, being visible to humans inhibits the pixies in their habitual thieving from us.[135]

A slightly curious, and possibly corrupted, story from Exmoor tells how a woman, "whose relative had dealings with the pixies" saw them stealing goods at Minehead market and was blinded by a pixie breathing in her eyes. Either there are key details missing here or, perhaps, the woman had handled some item that belonged to the pixies or had been in physical contact with her relative, who had acquired the power himself, thereby having the pixy-sight accidentally conferred upon her.[136]

The gift of pixy-sight may be acquired unintentionally. In Sennen, in Cornwall, the story was told of a woman who was preparing to bathe her baby. She put out warm water in readiness but, while she was in another room undressing the child, the pixies entered the house and washed their own children, assuming that the water had been left out for them. When the mother returned to bathe her baby, a little of the water splashed into her eyes and she immediately saw that the room around her was filled with the *pobel vean*. This clearly indicates that the 'glamour' can wash off the pixies and can then be physically transferred to others. When they appreciated what had happened, the pixies wanted to blind the woman but, in this case, she was reportedly able to escape from them with her sight intact.[137]

A green ointment which will reveal the pixies can be made from four leaf clover. Humans tend to encounter

---
[135] Tregarthen, *Folklore Tales*, 'Skerry Werry' and 'The Nurse Who Broke Her Promise,' (1940).
[136] Palmer, *Folklore of Somerset*, 22.
[137] Wentz, *Fairy Faith*, 182.

this when in the service of pixies, whether as midwifes, nurses or domestic servants, and accidentally touch their own eyes with it when they are supposed to be applying it to pixie babies. A few people know the secret of making it for themselves, however. Bottrell reported that the clover had to be gathered by the pixies; however, from elsewhere in Cornwall we hear about a green salve made from certain herbs that had been identified by the pixies on Kerris Moor, outside Paul, near Newlyn. In this particular case, the ointment bestowed invisibility when rubbed on the eyes, but in principle it seems that a human equipped with the right information and local knowledge ought to be able to assemble the ingredients and make the 'pixy-sight' salve.[138]

---

138 Tregarthen, *North Cornwall Fairies and Legends*, 167; Bottrell, *Traditions and Hearthside Stories*, vol.1, 209 and vol.2, 173 and 154; Wentz, *Fairy Faith*, 175.

CHAPTER SEVEN

Mischief

The pixies love practical jokes and will frequently trap and mislead people, but only for a while. Generally, it is said that they cause "a great deal of trouble and plague;" another writer put it more strongly, calling them "veritable little demons of mischief." Nonetheless, much of the behaviour of pixies must be regarded as naughtiness rather than malignity. The best advice, whatever they do, is to laugh at their pranks rather than to quarrel with them.[139]

Jonathan Couch said of the southern Cornish pixies that they are "interested in human affairs, now doing a good turn, now offending and causing mischief. They are the enemies of sluttery and encourage good husbandry." This remark highlights to us the possibly surprising fact that the pixies seem to have some highly defined moral values, which they apply to themselves *and* to the human population around them. As a result, much of what we might call misbehaviour may actually be retribution for violating their principles. There are, for example, said to be royal courts amongst the Dartmoor pixies, involving

---

[139] G. Herbert, 'Devonian Folklore Illustrated,' *Devonshire Association for the Advancement of Science, Literature and Art*, vol.2, 1867, 77; Wright, *Picturesque South Devonshire*, 16; Bowring, 'Devonshire Pixies,' *Once a Week Magazine*, vol.16, Jan.-June 1867, 204.

all the pleasure and luxury that you might anticipate. Yet, this hierarchy of monarchs and subjects is supported by law courts in which those who have offended pixie morality are punished by having to make ropes of sand – with which they're then bound. Meanwhile, those subjects who have pleased the pixie monarchs are rewarded with missions, which tend to involve playing amusing tricks on human kind.[140]

Pranks

The pixies indulge in a range of vexing but harmless pranks at the expense of their human neighbours.

An authority on Devonshire pixies listed an astonishing range of their practical jokes. They will pull away milking stools just as a maid is about to sit down, they may blow out candles and kiss girls in the dark and they may make noises down wells to alarm people. Readers may note that tricks like these are ascribed in the rest of England to Puck, or Robin Goodfellow. Amongst their other pranks, the pixies will spoil rennet, curdle milk, sour cider during storms, pull out the bungs in barrels, spilling the household's drink, drive the pigs into nettle patches, trip up horses in ditches, steal the vicar's sermon or tease shepherds by scattering their sheep, and then gathering them all together again.[141]

---

[140] J. Couch, *History of Polperro*, 133; Bowring, 'Devon Folklore,' 79.

[141] Bowring, 'Devonshire Pixies,' *Once a Week Magazine*, vol.16, Jan.-June 1867, 206; Bray, *Description*, 175. On Puck, see *Midsummer Night's Dream*, Act II, scene 1 and my *Famous Faeries*, 2020.

To the foregoing list a Cornish writer added that it was the habit "if the seamstress' thread is tangled, patches discomposed, thimbles lost, or domestic articles mislaid, to instantly blame piskays." William Bottrell recorded that the *bucca* liked to enter homes when cakes were baking in the oven, steal them, and replace them with turf. The housewives, who had been at the door talking to neighbours, would return to find only dark ashes and then would reproach themselves over how long they'd been absent. (It may be that we have some misogynistic sanctioning of gossips here). Nevertheless, any mishap that occurs in the kitchen overnight tended to be blamed upon the pixies.[142]

From Polperro on the Cornish south coast comes an example of the sort of pure nuisance behaviour that can so annoy the pixies' human victims. The little folk used to regularly call out to a man called Robin Hicks that his boat was adrift in the harbour, getting him out of bed in the middle of the night – only for him to find, of course, that there was no problem at all.[143]

Some pixie tricks seem clearly to arise from a moral indignation, as Jonathan Couch suggested. A trick of the Cornish pixies that's deployed against housewives or maid servants they don't like is to spoil bread in the oven, making it come out full of holes called 'pixy-spits.' In a specific example, one Cornish 'house-pixy' was so vexed by a farmer called Nicholas Annear who rushed and bullied his family and his labourers to get their work

---

[142] S. F. Hitchens, *History of Cornwall*, 1824, vol.1, 98; Wentz, *Fairy Faith*, 179; Bottrell, *Traditions and Hearthside Stories*, vol.1, 144.
[143] Quiller-Couch, 'Polperro,' *Notes and Queries*, vol.11, 397; J. Couch, *History of Polperro*, 136.

done that he chastened the man with a trick in order to reform his behaviour. Hurrying to market one day in his horse and cart, the farmer constantly saw a vision of the church tower ahead of him, but drive as hard as he might throughout the day, he never got any nearer, leaving him and his horse exhausted and sorry by evening. He was a reformed man after this, showing the pixies the respect due to them.[144]

Somerset pixies may combine mischief at humans' expense with help to wildlife. In one story told to folklorist Jon Dathen, the pixies give shelter inside a tree to an exhausted fox pursued by the horses and hounds of the local hunt. A moral disapproval of hunting for sport may be implied here.[145]

Riding Horses

The pixies are very fond of taking horses from stables at night and riding them. For instance, on the Somerset Levels near Brent Tor pixie riding is said to be a particular problem, with the horses being raced on the moorland at nights. On Dartmoor, apparently, it is particular fields that are more prone to pixie-riding than others; likewise, at Polperro, there was in the late 1860s a farmer who had learned not to put his horses in a certain field overnight, because they were always found to be sweating and terrified in the mornings. In North Cornwall, writer Enys Tregarthen ascribed this interference to the 'night riders,' whom she said were "a people no bigger than pixies" and

---

144 H. Harris *Cornish Saints and Sinners* (London: Clowes and Sons,1907) cc. 19 and 20.
145 Dathen *Somerset Fairies and Pixies* 22.

who were dressed in scarlet coats, green breeches and red caps. There seems very little reason for distinguishing them as a separate tribe or race from the rest of pixie-dom; nocturnal taking and riding of human horses is simply another pastime alongside dancing and entering human homes. Likewise, when Robert Hunt refers to the same riders as *buccas*, it only reminds us how loose the labels for the different types of pixie are and that we need not worry too much over precision.[146]

Pixies especially seem to love to annoy us by plaiting the manes and tails of horses at night, or by entangling them with burdock seed pods. These are an unsightly nuisance and the owner's inclination is to be rid of them as quickly as possible, but on Dartmoor it is believed to be bad luck to try to comb the hair smooth again. The only remedy is to cut the plait out, yet even when this has been done, it's said that the horses are spoiled after the experience. In 1867 a folklorist recorded that a Devon vet had seen pixie knots in the mane of a sick horse he had visited – plainly implying a causal connection between the two. Another Devonshire folklorist recorded an instance in 1898 which was taken as being similar proof. In December that year three knots were found to have been tied in the manes of three carthorses, leaving them "all of a twizzle." These knots were so tiny and tight that 'only' pixie fingers could have made them. The situation appears much the same in Cornwall. Whenever the ponies of Bodmin Moor were rounded up for sale at

---

[146] Crossing, Dartmoor Pixies, c.8; King, 'Folklore of Devonshire,' *Fraser's Magazine*, vol.8, 1873, 781; J. Couch, *History of Polperro*, 133; Tregarthen, *North Cornwall Fairies and Legends*, 39; Hunt, *Popular Romances*, vol.1, 87.

Summercourt Fair, they were found to have their manes badly tangled by the pixies.[147]

The manes aren't plaited just for nuisance value, though, but to fashion saddles and stirrups for up to twenty pixies to use at once – hence the name 'pisky-seat' given locally to the knots. Enys Tregarthen offered a variant upon this theme in her story *The Piskies on the Mare's Neck*. In her account, Josey Tregaskis is a farmer returning late from Camelford fair. He knows the risk of being 'piskey-laden' so he gallops home as fast as he can, hoping to evade any danger. This fails, because two piskies jump up on the horse with him, plaiting the horse's mane into stirrups and panniers as they ride.[148]

By some accounts, the horses may be ridden almost to death and are left distressed and off their food, but the animals don't necessarily object to this riding, either. Just as cattle seem to enjoy the pixies' company, there appears to be affection with horses too. According to one Somerset story, a horse was often observed to roll around in one corner of its field and then to gallop around to the sounds of laughter and play. After behaving like this for a while, the animal would settle back to grazing in silence. What was happening was only betrayed by a stirring of the grass nearby, which disclosed where the pixie who had ridden the steed was now walking away. Along the

---

147 King, 'Folklore of Devonshire,' *Fraser's Magazine*, vol.8, 1873, 781; Bowring, 'Devon Folklore,' 78 and 80; G. Herbert, 'Devonian Folklore Illustrated,' *Devonshire Association for the Advancement of Science, Literature and Art*, vol.2, 1867, 77; R. Northcote, 'Pixies in the Present Day,' *Devon Notes and Queries*, (1901), vol.1, no.20, 37; Deane and Shaw, *Folklore of Cornwall*, 91.
148 *Notes and Queries*, 1st series, vol.2, 1850, 475; Tregarthen, *Folklore Tales*, 'Piskies on the Mare's Neck,' (1940).

same lines, it is said that, when the pixies borrowed a farmer's team of old horses to move home away from the sound of Withypool church's bells, they were returned to him "look[ing] like beautiful two-year olds."[149]

Gallitraps

In Somerset the green pixie rings are called 'gallitraps' and we are told by Ruth Tongue that they are produced not by dancing but by the pixies riding colts in circles in the fields. If you step into one of these gallitraps, you are entirely within the pixies' power. If you have one foot in and one out, you can see them, but you can still escape.[150]

There's more to this phenomenon though. In several parishes in Devon the 'gallitrap' was a patch of land hedged about and considered uncanny. If any person who was 'feyed' (or fated) to be hung for a crime entered one of these fields, they would then be unable to leave again but would instead wander round in circles, searching vainly for the gate or stile, until the local parson was called to release them (thence into the custody of a magistrate). In this belief, many readers will identify the very close parallels between this process and the experience of being pixie-led, which will be discussed later in chapter eight. I can't help suspecting that the variant name *gallow-trap* may be a 'back formation' from *gallitrap*. People no longer understood the word, perhaps, but knew it was associated with stepping into a grassy ring and so devised the more prosaic legal explanation,

---

149 Hunt, *Popular Romances*, vol.1, 74; Mathews, *Tales of the Blackdown Borderland*, 61; Tongue, *Somerset Folklore*, 117.
150 *Somerset Folklore*, 1965, 115.

in which the supernatural is recruited to catch criminals.

Although this conception of the gallitrap seems some way away from the pixie rings discussed earlier in chapter five, they are intimately connected. In the story *Two Men of Mendip* by Walter Raymond, this scene occurs:

> "She held out her finger and traced upon the parched grass the greener round of a pixie ring. 'We be in a gallow-trap' she laughed. 'If either of us have a' done wrong, 'tis sure to be brought to light'. He started as if struck unawares, then with a low cry he hid his face in his hands... The superstition that any man of crime stepping into a fairy circle should surely come to justice was thrust out of her mind."[151]

Another dialect source confirms that in Somerset the word *'gyaalitrap'* referred to the familiar pixie-ring in meadows and pastures.

It therefore appears that, in south-west England, the idea of the gallitrap was steadily extended. Firstly, it came to signify any mysterious circle, shape or sign. Mary Palmer, a mid-eighteenth-century documenter of Devonshire dialect, recorded how one of her interviewees had watched the village parson in the wood to see if he "made any zerckles or gallytraps" – in other words, if he drew any shapes on the ground. It came about in time that gallytraps might be drawn inside, on tables, just as much as on the ground outside. In turn, once the word was associated more with odd shapes than with grassy rings, it began to be applied to anything that was a bit misshapen, so that in due course in Gloucestershire the

---
151 Raymond, *Two Men*, 1879, 230.

word was applied to frightful ornaments or head-dresses that people wore, or even to badly made tools.

It may also be worth noting that in Suffolk, in East Anglia, there is an apparition called the *gallytrot*. This is a white dog the size of a bullock that terrorises people at night. The name derives from the dialect verb *gally*, to frighten, and it may be a clue as to the real origin of this puzzling term, for we have already seen how terrifying it may be to be caught up in a pixie dance.

Abductions

> "See-saw Margery Daw,
>   Sold her bed and lay upon straw.
>   Sold her bed and lay upon hay;
>   Pisky came and took her away."[152]

Pixies can take people away, both temporarily and permanently. Such was their reputation for such kidnappings that, in Cornwall, naughty children used to be warned that "The piskies will carry you away if you do that again." Such children might then be said to be 'ill-wished.'[153]

A game-keeper and his wife living at Chudleigh, on Dartmoor, had two children, and one morning the eldest girl went out to play while her mother dressed her baby sister. In due course, the parents realised that the older child had disappeared and several days of frantic and fruitless searching followed, with help from their

---
152 C. Berry, *Cornwall*, 1949, 206.
153 Wentz, *Fairy Faith*, 174 and 183; Bottrell, *Traditions and Hearthside Stories*, vol.1, 39.

neighbours, and even bloodhounds. Eventually, after hope had nearly been lost, some young men went to pick nuts from a clump of trees near the keeper's house, and there they came suddenly on the child, completely undressed and without her clothes, but well and happy, not at all starved, and playing contentedly. The pixies were assumed to have stolen the child, but to have cared for her and returned her.[154]

A Cornish child abduction account also indicates that the experience need not be too distressing for the young victim. A boy from St Allen fell asleep in a wood and met a lady who took him to a wonderful underground cavern formed of crystal. He was missing for several days, but was eventually found, none the worse for his adventure.[155]

If the pixies have taken a liking to a particular child, often because of its prettiness, they can be persistent in their efforts to capture him or her. There is an account of a boy from St Just who was taken twice in one day – specified in the report as Christmas day, although this seems to have no special significance and would, on the face of it, be a day when the pixies might be anticipated to be *less* active in the human world. Each time, the boy was wrapped in a cloak and carried off, but managed to escape and return home after about an hour.[156]

Enys Tregarthen's story, *The Boy Who Played with Piskies,* may describe the preliminaries to an abduction, or shed a more benign light on the pixies. A lonely little boy living on St Columb moor wandered far and wide, having no-one to play with. One day he met a crowd of

---

154 Northcote, 'Devonshire Folklore', *Folklore*, vol.11, 1900, 213.
155 Deane and Shaw, *Folklore of Cornwall*, 94.
156 Bottrell, *Traditions and Hearthside Stories*, vol.1, 39; Wentz, *Fairy Faith*, 181

small people who let him play with them. They seem to have taken pity on his plight, but at the same time they instructed him to keep his new playmates secret from his mother. One day, though, she heard him laughing and later asked who he was playing with. He confessed that he had met pixies and, as a result of this breach of confidence, he never saw them again.[157]

Whilst they are a particular target, it is by no means solely children who are abducted. The saying is that the pixies "can't abear those whom they can't abide" and anyone who offends them may be taken and left abandoned on remote moorland away from their home. Sometimes, too, the abductee can be permanently affected by the experience and no longer feels settled in their former life.[158]

Just as with children, there is some indication that particular adults might be singled out for taking. The reasons for this are not clearly stated in the south-western sources like they are elsewhere in Britain, but it's probable that women are wanted as wives, wet nurses or servants and that men might be sought out for particular craft skills.[159] A brief rhyme recalled by one of Evans Wentz' witnesses, a man from Delabole, may represent a fragment of such a tradition. A pisky looked into a house and asked:

> "All alone, fair maid?
> No, here I am with a dog and cat,
> And apples to eat and nuts to crack."

---

[157] Tregarthen, *Folklore Tales*, 'The Boy Who Played with Piskies,' (1940).
[158] M. Courtney, *Cornish Feasts and Folklore*, 121.
[159] Hunt, *Popular Romances*, vol.1, 69.

The young woman is alone and possibly vulnerable, but she has a dog to protect her (in Scotland dogs often fight with fairies to protect their owners) as well, perhaps, as being alert and sharp-witted (again, in dealing with Highland faeries quick thinking and verbal dexterity can be essential). We only have three lines of verse, but the suggestion is that whatever the pixie's purpose may have been, the unafraid and confident response from the girl deflected it. Confirmation of this comes from Robert Hunt, who stated that "So wide-spread were their depredations, and so annoying their tricks, that it at one time was necessary to select persons whose acuteness and ready tact were a match for these quick-witted wanderers, and many a clever man has become famous for his power to give charms against Pigseys..."[160]

One of the best-known pixie abduction stories comes from Dartmoor. Some farm labourers were working in the fields near Dartmeet when they heard a voice repeatedly calling 'Jan Coo,' the name of one of the young farmhands. Deciding that it had to be the pixies they could hear (because it was a location notorious for being frequented by the little folk) the men decided to pay no attention, especially when they found that a response caused the shouting to stop. The boy, however, was drawn by the calls, which seemed each day to get louder. Jan thought the voice was coming from a deep pool in the river and he entered the water there – and was never seen again.[161]

The Jan Coo story is particularly interesting because it suggests a link to water. We saw earlier, in chapter four,

---

160 Wentz, *Fairy Faith*, 184; Hunt, *Popular Romances*, vol.1, 67.
161 Crossing, *Dartmoor Pixies*, c.7.

the tradition that pixie-land could be entered through bogs and quick sands by rivers. Near Tamerton, in north east Cornwall, there is a lake surrounded by a sandy shore where, if you step on the wrong section of the strand, you will be taken by the pixies. All of these spots may be regarded as 'liminal' locations that connect different dimensions, bridging the gap between this middle earth and the pixie world.[162]

Changelings

As well as being taken for a limited period of time, children may sometimes be abducted permanently, with the pixies leaving behind a decoy or substitute, known as a changeling. The pixie replacement is typically *wisht-looking* or *winickey,* that is – withered, weak, frail and peevish – yet with a voracious appetite. Of such children it is said that they "don't goodey" or thrive and, as such, they are easily identified. For obvious reasons, efforts are then usually made by the parents to seek the restoration of their own child. Ideally, this has to be done very quickly. A correspondent of Robert Hunt informed him that "I never knew but one child that had been kept by the Spriggans more than three days. It was always complaining, sickly, and weakly, *and had the very face of a changeling.*"[163]

Although nowadays we have developed a generally beneficent and indulgent view of pixies, it's fascinating to learn that in the past they were regarded as being

---

[162] 'Pixies of Devonshire,' *Newcastle Courant*, Dec.25th 1846, 3.
[163] Wentz, *Fairy Faith*, 177 and 179; Couch, *History of Polperro*, 133; Hunt, *Popular Romances*, vol.1, 72.

a very serious threat because of their habit of stealing children. "Devonshire is, above all other lands, the land of changeling boys and girls" one writer declared – which he proved by mentioning an old woman he'd been told about when he was a boy who had talked like a fifty-year-old from the age of five. A contemporary of this writer felt that in Victorian times there was a changeling to be found in every Dartmoor village. The women of Bishopsteignton were notoriously very small, and this was believed to be because they were descended from changelings. Similarly, in 1846, it was stated that there was a woman currently living in Totnes who was a pixie changeling. So common were such kidnappings that mothers locally would pin their babies to their sides to try to protect them or would leave a prayer book under the babies' pillows (not always successfully).[164]

If the preventative measures failed, the parent would have to take steps to recover their child. An illustration of the extremes to which some people went is a woman called Jenny Trayer who lived near Carn Euny in Penwith. She had her child taken – and this despite employing one of the recommended precautions: she had crossed the (iron) fire hook and the furze prong on the hearth. The child left behind was forever crying and always hungry, yet it only got thinner as time passed. Jenny was advised that the cure was to dip the changeling infant

---

164 J. Bowring, "Devonshire Pixies," *Once a Week*, vol.16 (1867) 205; Northcote, 'Devonshire Folklore,' 213; Richard King, 'The Folklore of Devonshire,' in *Fraser's Magazine*, vol.8, 1873, 781; R. Northcote, 'Pixies in the Present Day,' *Devon Notes and Queries*, (1901), vol.1, no.20, 38; 'Pixies of Devonshire,' *Newcastle Courant*, Dec.25th 1846 ,3; *Notes and Queries*, 1st series, vol.2, December 1850.

in Chapel Euny well on the first three Wednesdays in May, turning the child round three times from west to east – or anticlockwise, against the sun. On the third trip to the well, Jenny was scared off by a disembodied voice addressing her – to which her changeling child responded. The ability of changelings to behave like adults is another key indicator of their real nature.[165]

This method having been thwarted, Jenny was advised to place the child on her ash pile and to beat it with a broom; then she was to place it naked overnight under a church stile. This worked and her baby was duly returned to her, well washed and wrapped in a clean cloth. However, he was never 'right' after that and spent most of his time tending cattle before dying at only thirty.[166]

Very commonly, infants were snatched from their cradles, but sometimes mothers were attacked outside. A North Cornish woman was out digging potatoes in a field with her baby when they were caught by a whirlwind of dust. Once it had passed, she saw that her child was now a wizened old creature – which, despite her best efforts, pined away and died within a year.[167]

Other means of driving off a pixie changeling were to lay a four-leaf clover upon the child, to expose it outdoors overnight or to make a smoky fire of green bracken, fill the house with smoke, and then go outside and turn

---

[165] Chapel Euny well had an established reputation for healing childhood sicknesses. Bathing took place at the start of May and involved dipping the child three times and dropping a pin in the well (William Borlase, *Natural History of Cornwall*, 1757, 31; J. O. Halliwell-Phillipps, *Rambles in Western Cornwall by the Footsteps of the Giants*, 1861; Dr. Paris, *Guide to Mount's Bay*, 82).
[166] Bottrell, *Traditions and Hearthside Stories*, vol.2, 200.
[167] Tregarthen, *North Cornwall Fairies and Legends*, 185.

around three times. In each case, the changeling would depart and the original child would then reappear. Passing the changeling through the holed central stone of the *Men an Tol* in Penwith was also believed to be efficacious, because the 'good' pixie there could undo the work of the 'bad' pixies.[168]

One Dartmoor woman had her child taken whilst she was putting out her washing on the line. She was, naturally, deeply upset, but decided to care for the changeling child as well as she had cared for her own. The pixies seemed to appreciate this, because they returned her child in due course and the infant grew up always to be lucky in life.[169]

Most of the children taken are, sadly, rarely seen again. A strange exception to this occurred at the pixie fair at Germoe. The witness, one Daniel Champion, was sure he saw his own beautiful child there, only a few nights after his infant had been changed to an ugly and wizened creature. This, of course, was not something the pixies would have wished him to see and their response was typical. The next day he just in the process of telling the story to a workmate when the man had a fall and was killed. Carrying the man's body to his home, Champion started telling his story again and one of the pall bearers quickly warned him not to speak of the pixies because they were such "wicked, spiteful devils." Nonetheless, this man immediately had a fall as well and was bruised dreadfully.[170]

---

168 Wentz, *Fairy Faith*, 171, 177 and 179; Courtney, *Cornish Feasts and Folklore*, 126; Bottrell, *Traditions and Hearthside Stories*, vol.2, 202.
169 Bray, *Description*, 177.
170 Hunt, *Popular Tales*, vol.1, 86.

MISCHIEF

As has been said, female changelings seemed to be very widespread in Devon. A Dartmoor example was Grace Townsend, the sister of Jimmy. He always swore that his sibling had been changed by the pixies when he was a young boy. Nonetheless she grew into her twenties and was a healthy and marriageable young woman, whatever her brother had to say. In due course she married, although Jimmy warned that the union was unlikely to be happy. At first his forecasts seem to be disproved, but then Grace's new husband lost his cow, followed by his litter of pigs and then his geese. He was forced to give up farming, but every other line of work he tried was cursed with misfortune as well – a run of bad luck that Jimmy and others locally took as proof that the man had chosen a pixie wife.[171]

It appears that many parents simply accepted the pixie child, perhaps because they didn't want to resort to the sort of violent measures tried by Jenny Trayer. In 1873 poet Elias Tozer remarked upon the recent death of a tiny woman at Moreton who was reputed to have been a changeling, brought up by the human parents as their own after their original child was stolen. It seems to have been quite common for the human mother to care for the sickly or disabled pixie infant for as much as a couple of decades before it died. It is likely that this was done in the hope that the pixies would notice and reward this devotion: for instance, in the case of a changeling child at Breage, it was said that the pixies regularly visited the cottage to check on its well-being. Given their vengeful

---

[171] Bowring, 'Devonshire Pixies,' *Once a Week*, vol.16 (1867), 205; Crossing, *Tales of Dartmoor Pixies* c.5.

reputation, it's understandable that parents would have wished not to annoy them.[172]

In contrast to these sombre accounts, there is also a little evidence of pixie concern for the welfare of human children. Betty Stogs lived in the 'high countries' of Penwith, around Morva, Zennor and Towednack. She and her husband were poor, drunken and negligent parents, but the pixies intervened. They removed the infant, washed its clothes and left it near the cottage covered in flowers. This was an act of kindness, but also one intended to reform the neglectful mother.[173]

Fighting

Although they are known for their mischievous pranks, the pixies are not usually thought of as warlike but, like many British faeries, they do have a ferocious and combative side to their characters.

A Cornish woman called Emlyn Moyle was pixie-led in the fog on Goss Moor. She found herself near to the ancient hillfort, Castle an Dinas, and saw a pixie battle being fought upon the ramparts. When the fog cleared, though, there was no trace of any fighting there. This is not an isolated incident: it's been said that the pixies only gained control of Devonshire after a protracted war with the elves. Now, however, everything west of the River Parrett is 'pixie-land.'[174]

---

172 Bray, *Description*,177; Tozer, *Devonshire and Other Original Poems*, 81; Wentz, *Fairy Faith*, 171.
173 Hunt, *Popular Romances of the West of England*.
174 E. Tregarthen, *Pixie Folklore and Legends*, (New York, Gramercy Books, 1996) 67–75; Bray, *Peeps on Pixies*, 12; Tongue, *Somerset Folklore*, 112.

The fierce and martial temperament of the Cornish spriggans is seen in the tale of *The Fairies of the Eastern Green*. One night some smugglers landed their illicit cargo of brandy at Longrock Beach, on Mount's Bay between Penzance and Marazion. One of the crew went ashore to investigate some mysterious sounds, fearing it was the excise men lying in wait. Instead, he stumbled upon a large number of spriggans, dressed in red and green and enjoying a dance in the sand dunes. As soon as they realised that they had been discovered, the crowd of dancers turned nasty and chased the smuggler with spears, slings and bows. He raced back to his boat, calling on his companions to put out to sea again. The spriggans swarmed angrily onto the beach but could not harm the boat on the waves because "none of the faery tribe dare touch salt water."[175]

Smuggling

In the last story cited, human smugglers are attacked by pixies. Cornish fairy tale writer Enys Tregarthen recorded a curious account of woman from Newtrain Bay near Padstow which suggests that the *pobel vean* may have been smugglers themselves. This woman knew very well that the local pixies used to dance on the cliff tops in the moonlight but one night, instead of finding them there, she encountered them coming up from the beach carrying bags, which they told her were their beds. Neither she, nor Tregarthen, comment upon this incident, but the plain implication seems to be that these pixies had, in fact, been involved in importing contraband tobacco or

---

175 Bottrell, *Stories and Folklore of West Cornwall*, 93.

something similar. Other than their presence in mines, the little folk mostly seem to subsist by stealing from humans, so this short tale casts an interesting new light on their economic activities.[176]

Weather

Robert Hunt stated that the spriggans in particular caused storms, lightning and bad weather and were responsible for natural disasters. The Cornish pixies are also able to control the mists and fogs. These powers can be used to protect buried gold or to play pranks and mislead travellers and, as we saw just now, human babies can be carried off in whirlwinds.[177] You may recall from chapter one that William Borlase suggested that the pixies were ancient spirits of nature; their control of the weather may substantiate this idea.

Protections

Given the multiple threats that pixies can pose to the human population, it's inevitable that a range of protective measures were developed to keep them away. We have already seen some being used to defend babies against abduction; but they are of general application.

Bread somehow works to protect people from the *pobel vean*. It is widely believed throughout Britain that carrying a crust is a sure way of protecting yourself from

---

176 Tregarthen, *North Cornwall Fairies and Legends*, 179.
177 Hunt, *Popular Romances*, 81; Bottrell, *Traditions and Hearthside Stories*, vol.1, 49; M. E. Whitcomb, *Bygone Days in Devon and Cornwall*, 149.

malign influence, especially from being pixie-led. Stuart poet Robert Herrick wrote that:

> "If ye feare to be affrighted,
>   When ye are (by chance) benighted,
>   In your pocket for a trust
>   Carrie nothing but a Crust:
>   For that holy piece of Bread,
>   Charmes the danger, and the dread."

Herrick was vicar of Dean Prior in Devon and would have been very familiar with local superstitions and practices. The verse seems to imply that, originally, people must have carried a piece of consecrated host, but eventually any sort of bread was thought to be as good. Other effective measures include having iron or a Christian text about you, crossing your fingers and carrying a cross made of 'wicken' (rowan).[178]

Iron implements are an especially good protection against the risk of a child being exchanged, but even something as everyday as wearing hob-nailed boots may safeguard the individual. Whistling also seems to be a good defence – and we may recall the knockers' objection to miners whistling below ground that was mentioned earlier in chapter five.[179]

---

178 Tongue, *Somerset Folklore*, 113.
179 K. Briggs, *Dictionary of Fairies*, under 'Pixy-led' or in *The Fairies in Tradition and Literature*, 1968, 138–139; also see Bord, *Fairies*, 15

CHAPTER EIGHT

Pixie Leading

The commonest pixie prank, or sanction, is the practice known as pixie-leading – deliberately getting a person lost at night. Leading astray on purpose is a fairy habit almost exclusively found in South West Britain. It is reported about as often in Cornwall and Devon, with about twenty-five per cent of cases taking place in other counties (Dorset and Somerset) and slightly fewer in Wales. Pixie-leading is a practice that has been recorded for many centuries.

We have already seen that poet Robert Herrick, writing in the first half of the 1600s, advised carrying bread "If ye feare to be affrighted/ When ye are (by chance) benighted." He was pretty clearly alluding to the risk of pixie-leading. A second Devonshire poet, the Puritan Christopher Clobery, who wrote in 1659, more explicitly warned of "fairy elves who thee mislead … in to the mire, then at thy folly smile/ Yea, clap their hands for joy." The remedy he advised was identical to Herrick's: "Old country folk, who pixie-leading fear/ Bear bread about them, to prevent harm."

Methods

To be pixie-led is a very well-known phrase, but what does it actually entail? There are, in fact, at least half a

PIXIE LEADING

dozen different experiences which are classed under this heading.

Using glamour so that the human victim no longer recognises where they are is the commonest way to confuse and lead astray a person. A few accounts will exemplify this: *Once a Week* magazine in 1867 reported how a young farmer was pixie-led one evening in an orchard – where he was trapped for two hours. Comparably, a Cornish man called Glasson, whilst making the short walk from Ludgvan to Gulval near Penzance, found himself completely lost and going in circles, until he turned his coat – and heard a peal of high-pitched laughter. In both these cases, and more, a familiar place – often of very small extent – became strange; land marks disappeared and panic set in.[180]

Sometimes, the change made is to conceal the gate out of a field. Often, again, the enclosed space is very familiar to the victim and the moon may be shining, but the means of escape seem to vanish. To add to this, in several Cornish accounts the pixies also frustrate their victims' attempts to get free by raising the field hedge whenever they find a lower section that they might have been able to climb over. This kind of treatment leaves the victim 'mizzy-mazey' and unable to think calmly and recall how to save themselves.[181]

The pixies are known for their ability to control the weather and this can be used very effectively as a way of

---

[180] Bowring, 'Devonshire Pixies,' *Once a Week Magazine*, vol.16, Jan.-June 1867, 608; Deane and Shaw, *Folklore of Cornwall*, 90.
[181] Bottrell, *Hearthside Stories*, vol.1, 57; Enys Tregarthen, *Folklore Tales*, 'The Enchanted Field' (1911) or 'How Jan Brewer was Pisky Laden,' in *North Cornwall Fairies and Legends*, 151; Tongue, *Somerset Folklore*, 113.

trapping victims. Men travelling across Dartmoor from Crediton or South Molton to Exeter were advised that, if a cloud descended, they should strip and sit on their clothes for half an hour or so. The pixies would in due course raise the fog thrown around them and the spell would dissipate. Patience is evidently important in such cases. A woman on the Quantocks became demented with terror when the pixies caused an evening mist to rise suddenly around her, so that she was lost in a field minutes away from her home. On the Cornish moors as well, the pixies are said to conjure fog purely to lead travellers astray.[182]

Just as a person may become trapped in a familiar field, they may (as we have already seen) step into a pixie ring and fall into their power. A Somerset farmer coming home from market was led like this until he ended up exhausted by a briar bush that grew in three counties – a plant that seems to have broken the spell he was under. Cornish fairy author Enys Tregarthen has called the rings 'Spriggan Traps.'[183]

Perhaps related to this phenomenon is that of following a 'piskey-path.' Enys Tregarthen also described how these mysterious green paths can be seen on cliffs or meandering across the moors, still verdant when the bracken is dry and brown. On Dartmoor there are many intricate paths that are called 'pixie lanes,' places where it is easy to lose your way. Writing in 1630 in his *View of Devonshire,* Thomas Westcote mentioned how a person

---

182 V. C. Clinton-Baddeley, *Devon*, 100; Whistler, 'Local Traditions of the Quantocks,' *Folklore*, vol.19, 48; Crofton Croker, *Fairy Legends*, vol.3, vi; Bottrell, *Traditions and Hearthside Stories*, vol 1, 48; Hunt *Popular Romances* vol.2, 245 and vol.1, 48.
183 Tongue, *Somerset Folklore*, 114.

who got lost on Dartmoor would be "led in a pixy-path." Here there is some definite, albeit unclear, link between the paths and being pixie-led.[184]

Lastly, the pixies may lure people away from their route with music, thereby getting them lost. This has been reported in Devon. Night time travellers can also be distracted from their route by seeing lights, whether these are moving about or appear to be coming from a nearby house or hostelry. In other parts of Britain, the supernaturals that appear as moving lights are often called wills of the wisp or Jack o' Lanterns. In the southwest, they are frequently termed 'pixy-lights' instead. It's also worth recalling that the Pucks and Pooks of the English Midlands and South Wales can often act like a will of the wisp, so that there seems to be a clear connection between these spirits' names.[185]

Motivations

Who do the pixies mislead humans? They seem to have several motivations. Above all, there's their love of mischief; they need no reason as such, other than the pleasure in mildly tormenting us – which gives them great amusement. They are often said to be heard laughing or, even, clapping their hands with glee at their victim's torment. They might sometimes be seen jumping about in front of the victim, mocking their situation.[186]

---

[184] V. C. Clinton-Baddeley, *Devon*, 99; Tregarthen, *Pisky Purse*, 1905.
[185] See for example, Wirt Sikes, *British Goblins*, 23; see too my *Beyond Faery*, 2020.
[186] Evans Wentz, *Fairy Faith*, 184.

Whatever the entertainment value of leading someone, though, the pixies may simultaneously feel that the person needs to be punished for some reason. If they have been insulted by a person, s/he will be targeted in revenge – and then "their malevolence knows no ends."[187]

In Somerset, it was believed that the pixies used to lead people astray as a way of demonstrating their moral disapproval over cheating at market, laziness, stealing or drunkenness. A man from Bishop's Lydeard in the Quantock Hills picked up a pixy grindstone as he was out walking and decided to keep it. A mist descended upon him and he was led through brambles all night. A woman from Selworthy parish on the Exmoor coast of Somerset saw a group of pixies; they were so upset by her intrusion that they led her all over the moor and through the woods. As we know, any trespass upon the fairies' privacy is bitterly resented. In one Cornish story a man was pisky-laden by disappearing gates because he had been obstinate and denied the pixies' existence.[188]

Reactions

As for the human victims, how do they react? Inevitably, they will end up exhausted, frustrated and panic-stricken. They are often said, in Devon, to be 'mazed' as a result, a neat term that is suggestive of being both amazed and lost (in a maze).[189]

The consequences of being pixie-led can be much more serious, though; the experience can cause terror

---

187 Page, *An Exploration of Dartmoor*, 37.
188 Tongue, *Somerset Folklore*, 114–115; Tregarthen, *Folklore Tales*, 'Why Jen Pendogget Changed his Mind' (1940).
189 Wright, *Picturesque South Devonshire*, 16.

and a loss of wits. A man who was pixie-led on the Blackdown Hills in Somerset had to be rescued after he was lured into a bog. He was ill for quite some time after this experience. A Devonshire man crossing Dartmoor near Chudleigh was pixie-led by the sound of music. He wandered for hours, trying to locate the source, and eventually collapsed in a faint. When he came round the next morning, he was able to make his way home, but he took to his bed, never rose again and soon afterwards died. A Somerset man returning from the pub who found himself misled and lost was rescued by a local farmer who heard his cries of distress. In response to the experience, the man worked for his saviour for free, helping on the farm as well as road making. He said that he did this to please the pixies, so that they wouldn't give him a "gude lammin'" the next time they came across him alone at night. This strongly suggests some sense of pixie-leading being used as a means of moral reform.[190]

The most extreme outcome is one from Somerset in which a farmer from Hangley Cleave was pixy-led because he was a drunk who wasted his money and mistreated his wife and children. One foggy night as he rode home drunk, he saw a light in the mist and headed towards it, thinking it was his house. Too late he realised that it was actually a pixie holding a lantern over one of the deepest bogs in the area. The farmer's horse refused to go further so the man jumped off, straight into the mire, into which he sank without trace. When the old horse arrived home alone, the family realised what had

---

190 *Notes and Queries*, 1850, no.61, 511; Mathews, *Tales of the Blackdown Borderland*, 58 and 62.

happened and ever after swept the hearth and left out clean water at nights for the pixies.[191]

Remedies

If you *are* pixie-led, what can you do to free yourself? There are several tried and tested remedies.

The best known and easiest remedy is to turn an item of clothing – a hat might be turned back to front, a coat, pocket, glove or stocking might be turned inside out. Even simply turning a coin over inside your pocket can be effective. There are two stories in which throwing a glove banished the pixies: whether this is somehow related is not entirely clear. It seems likely that turning clothes is effective because it changes your appearance and throws the pixies off the scent, although Mrs Bray proposed, rather primly and feebly, that the pixies were driven away because they objected to disorderly dress. It's worth adding, though, that in Enys Tregarthen's story *The Pisky Who Rode in a Pocket,* a pixie's presence in the victim's clothing is the cause of their wandering astray – and the spell is only broken when she turns out her pockets, thereby ejecting the mischievous passenger.[192]

Wise travellers turn their clothes *before* they set out, so that they will be safe from enchantment throughout their journey. It appears that for residents of areas like Dartmoor or Exmoor, the risk of being pixie-led was

---

191 Tongue, *Somerset Folklore*, 114; see too Briggs, *Dictionary of Fairies*, under 'Pixies.'
192 Tozer, *Devonshire and Other Original Poems*, 76; Bray, *Description*, 183; Wentz, *Fairy Faith*, 183; Tregarthen, *Folklore Tales*, 'The Pisky Who Rode in a Pocket,' (1940). For throwing gloves see *The House on Silena Moor* and Hunt's 'St Leavan Fairies,' recounted earlier.

accepted as being an everyday hazard, rather like the risk that you might get caught by a shower of rain, and it was something for which they prepared habitually. Poet Elias Tozer recalled a nurse from Gidleigh who was regularly led astray. She simply accepted it, knowing that all she had to do was to turn out her pockets to be safe again. Likewise, near Camelford in North Cornwall there was an area called 'pixy-hell' where misleading was normal for the traveller; locals would always turn out their pockets before venturing that way.[193]

Attracting the attention of other people who've not fallen under the pixie spell will work to free a person. This is effective in two ways. Either the rescuer calls out in reply to help guide the victim to safety or the pixie-led person makes a noise which attracts rescuers to where she or he is stranded. For instance, Abraham Stocke in Somerset had said that he had no time for stories of pixies and definitely wasn't scared of them. One night when he was walking home from band practice, he fell into the hedge several times and then, seeing lights, was led into a swamp. Luckily, he had his euphonium with him and was able to play it to alert his family and guide them to him. They were then able to haul him out of the bog with a rope, but even after this he felt unwell. He was advised to turn his pockets to feel better; he turned his hat instead and improved, but was still sick for a period of time afterwards.[194]

Additionally, it looks from the cases as though a person simply coming along and startling the victim out of

---

193 Tozer, *Devonshire and Other Original Poems*, 81; Hammond, *A Cornish Parish – St Austell*, 360; R. Pearse Chope, 'Folklore of Devon,' *London Devonian Yearbook*, 1910, 112.
194 Mathews, *Tales of the Blackdown Borderland*, 58 and 62.

their bemusement can often be enough to release them. Equally, the evidence suggests that the mere appearance of another human can be enough disturb the pixies, or to break their spell. A passer-by, who is not caught up in the enchantment, is sufficient to dispel the glamour and restore reality.[195]

It can help to carry something with you to protect you against pixie charms during your travels. This could be a cross made from rowan wood, a piece of bread (as we've seen already) or a sprig of the plant greater stitchwort. Rowan, or mountain ash, is well-known for repelling supernaturals beings of all kinds (witches included). The stitchwort is more unusual and seems to be a uniquely Devonian remedy. The flower is called 'pixies' in the county and it is believed to be the special property of the little people. Picking it will upset them, but apparently carrying it with you somehow has the effect of deflecting rather than attracting their ill-will.

Water (as often with fairies) can release the bewildered person. Drinking the water from Fitz's Well, near Okehampton on the northern edge of Dartmoor, dispels the glamour cast by the local pixies. In addition, any running water may have the same effect and, in fact, it is possible that merely falling into a stream might be sufficient to break the spell, as the next story shows. One day at the very beginning of June, 1890, a man from Torrington in North Devon was working in a wood. At the end of the day, he became separated from his companions when he went to collect a tool he had left

---

[195] K. Briggs, *Dictionary of Fairies*, under 'Pixy-led' or in *The Fairies in Tradition and Literature*, 1968, 138–139; also see Bord, *Fairies*, 15.

nearby. On bending down to pick it up, a strange feeling came over him; he found that he was unable to move and, at the same time, he could hear the pixies laughing. He realised he was at their mercy. When the man had not returned home by ten o'clock that night, his wife became very alarmed and went out to look for him. She met her husband emerging from the wood, soaked to the skin. He explained he had been held under the pixies' spell for nearly five hours, capable only of crawling along on his hands and knees. It was dark and he had no idea where he was, as a result of which he fell into a stream, but this accident luckily had the beneficial effect of dispelling the enchantment. The wood was apparently known for pixie-leading, although this is not really the right term for the man's experience, which was much more akin to a paralysis.[196]

Lastly, some cases indicate that the mere passage of time is all that's needed. If the victim of being "stogged in the mux" is patient, the daylight will come, the pixies' power will dissipate and they will be able to escape.[197]

As soon as victims have gathered their wits and have applied one of the countermeasures, the pixies will promptly abandon their game. They depart with a peal of mocking laughter, which only serves to underline the fact that the person has been pixie-led.

---

[196] '11th Report on Devonshire Folklore,' *Transactions of the Devonshire Association for the Advancement of Science*, vol.24, 1892, 52, reproducing a report in the *Western Daily Mercury*, June 6th 1890.
[197] Bowring, 'Devonshire Pixies,' *Once a Week Magazine*, vol.16, Jan-June 1867, 204.

Summary

People may be pixie-led merely for the amusement of the little folk, or the prank may also be intended as a sanction or warning. If you are the subject of a pixie-leading, two things are important. The first is to try to calm yourself, analyse your situation and use one of the remedies. The second, subsequently, will be to consider whether or not you may have offended the pixies in some way. The majority of leadings are mere pranks, but some have serious intent and it follows that it's both wise and respectful to reflect upon this possibility.

CHAPTER NINE

Fading Belief?

Even as early as 1824 some writers were foretelling the end of the pixies. One history of Cornwall lamented that "the age of piskays, like that of chivalry, is gone. There is perhaps at present hardly a house they are reputed to visit... The fields and lanes are forsaken. Their music is rarely heard." By then, it was only the aged and the unenlightened who still believed.[198] Plainly the author reckoned without the impact of Mrs Bray's books, which began to appear from 1836 onwards.

Researching Devon folklore mid-century, Sir John Bowring interviewed four old peasants on Dartmoor who assured him that "the piskies had all gone now, although there had been many formerly." Despite this, he was simultaneously told a version of the common story of pixies caught stealing grain from a barn, something that had apparently happened as recently as three years before. Another writer in the same year also asserted that belief was fading. Describing the same region a few decades later, John Page repeated the claim that "Faith in the elfin race is growing weaker by the day... The pixies are departing from Dartmoor." However, William Crossing in 1890 explained that, rather than disappearing, the

---

198 F. Hitchens, *History of Cornwall from the Earliest Records*, 1824, vol.1, 98.

pixies had become more retiring than they had been previously and that, as a result of fewer sightings, belief was fading, although it still lingered here and there. In 1903 Frederick Snell declared pixie belief on Exmoor to be "very faint." These claims notwithstanding, William Bottrell in 1873 said that "belief in fairies is far from being extinct in Cornwall." Clearly, it depended who you spoke to.[199]

Despite these prognostications, there is plentiful evidence that the pixies continue to thrive. The human tendency seems always to assume that *real* belief passed away with their grandparents' generation and that only a shadow of this survives in their present. So it was that in the early 1960s, a writer was in two minds whether true belief persisted on Dartmoor. On the one hand she felt it was only incomers who liked to keep the stories alive, and that the genuine faith of local inhabitants had died out centuries before, with only the commercial souvenir pixie surviving, catering for the tourist trade. On the other hand, she still heard from time to time of sightings and of respectful conduct maintained. She had been told that, as recently as the 1950s, milk was still put out overnight for the pixies on one Dartmoor farm.[200]

Other writers continue to affirm the irrepressible vitality of the pixies. Modern sightings are still reported;

---

[199] J. Bowring, "Devon Folklore Illustrated," *Transactions of the Devonshire Association*, vol.II (1867) 70; G. Herbert, 'Devonian Folklore Illustrated,' *Devonshire Association for the Advancement of Science, Literature and Art*, vol.2, 1867, 77; Crossing, *Tales of Dartmoor Pixies* cc.1 and 4; Page *Dartmoor* 40; Snell, *Book of Exmoor*, 248; Bottrell, *Traditions and Hearthside Stories*, vol.2, 245.

[200] R. St. Leger Gordon, *The Witchcraft and Folklore of Dartmoor*,1965, 16 and 21.

our understanding of the complex nature and character of the pixies continues to evolve. We still want and need them to animate our countryside – and the pixies have no intention of going anywhere soon.[201]

---

201 Dathen *Somerset Fairies and Pixies*, 2010; M. Johnson, *Seeing Fairies*, 2014.

Further Reading

Many of these books are readily available on line or in book form in cheap modern reprints.

William Bottrell, *Traditions and Hearthside Stories,* (two volumes), 1870; *Stories and Folklore of West Cornwall,* 1880;
Katharine Briggs, *A Dictionary of Fairies,* 1977;
Robert Hunt, *Popular Romances of the West of England,* (two volumes),1903;
Walter Evans Wentz, *The Fairy Faith in Celtic Countries,* 1911.

The foregoing sources deal with pixie beliefs of the nineteenth century and before. Two very important modern books are:

Jon Dathen *Somerset Fairies and Pixies,* 2010;
Marjorie Johnson, *Seeing Fairies,* 2014.

www.ingramcontent.com/pod-product-compliance
Ingram Content Group UK Ltd.
Pitfield, Milton Keynes, MK11 3LW, UK
UKHW022354081025
463742UK00004B/21